SARAJEVO

A WAR JOURNAL

Zlatko Dizdarević

SARAJEVO

A WAR JOURNAL

PREFACE BY JOSEPH BRODSKY
INTRODUCTION BY ROBERT JAY LIFTON

Translated from the French
by Anselm Hollo

Edited from the original Serbo-Croatian
by Ammiel Alcalay

An Owl Book
Henry Holt and Company
New York

The publisher gratefully acknowledges the help of Ammiel Alcalay,
Salko Krijestorac, and Alan Fogelquist in the publication of this book.

Henry Holt and Company, Inc.
Publishers since 1866
115 West 18th Street
New York, NY 10011

Henry Holt ® is a registered trademark of
Henry Holt and Company, Inc.

Published in Canada by Fitzhenry & Whiteside Ltd.,
195 Allstate Parkway, Markham, Ontario L3R 4T8.

Library of Congress Cataloging-in-Publication Data
Dizdarević, Zlatko.
[Journal de guerre.   English]
Sarajevo : a war journal / Zlatko Dizdarević ; preface by Joseph Brodsky ;
introduction by Robert Jay Lifton ; translated from the French by Anselm Hollo ;
edited from the original Serbo-Croatian by Ammiel Alcalay. — 1st Owl Book ed.
p.   cm.
"An Owl Book."
Originally published in English under title: Sarajevo under siege.
New York : Fromm International, 1993.
1. Sarajevo (Bosnia and Hercegovina—History—Siege, 1992–   —Personal
narratives, Bosnian. 2. Dizdarević, Zlatko—Diaries. I. Hollo, Anselm. II. Title.
DR1313.32. S27D5913   1994   94-26222
949.7'42—dc20   CIP

ISBN 0-8050-3535-4

CONTENTS

Preface by Joseph Brodsky ix

Introduction by Robert Jay Lifton xv

Maps xxvii

25 June 1993 Madness Against Reason 3

25 April 1992 Bosnian Roulette 9

1 May 1992 When Liberators Occupy Truth 12

8 May 1992 Dirty Politics 15

10 May 1992 To Leave or to Stay 18

16 May 1992 Bad News 21

17 May 1992 Lana's Childhood 24

18 May 1992 Life Suspended by a Thread 27

2 June 1992 Tennis—Life and Death 30

7 June 1992 Children and Blocks of Wood 33

10 June 1992 The Logic of Chaos 36

12 June 1992 On New Horizons 39

CONTENTS

13 June 1992 Spring in Sarajevo 42

17 June 1992 Mojmilo, the Hill of Accusation 45

18 June 1992 The "Un-Protection Force" 48

19 June 1992 No Forgiveness for Humiliation 52

20 June 1992 A Nice Sunny Day 55

21 June 1992 *Oslobodenje* in Flames 58

25 June 1992 The Long Goodbye 61

26 June 1992 A Word of Honor 64

27 June 1992 Straw Dogs 67

29 June 1992 The Spare Wheel 70

1 July 1992 Eyes and Ears 73

2 July 1992 Canned Goods 77

3 July 1992 Kind People 80

4 July 1992 The Flies and the Werewolves 83

5 July 1992 The Yellow High Rise 86

6 July 1992 The "Liberation" of Grbavica 89

8 July 1992 Bosnian Stomach Trouble 92

11 July 1992 City Around the Corner 95

12 July 1992 An Encounter with the Future 98

CONTENTS

3 October 1992 Learning by Wounds and Lies 144

3 November 1992 Ministers of Distant Affairs 147

5 November 1992 Video Letter from Paris 151

13 July 1992 One Hundred Days of Solitude 101

14 July 1992 A Long Hot Summer 104

17 July 1992 The Game of Absurdity 107

18 July 1992 The Lions in the Lion Cemetery 110

21 July 1992 Denial of a Mandate for Life 113

27 July 1992 Smart Bosnians and Dumb Bosnians 116

30 July 1992 Lord, Victims, and Zombies 119

7 August 1992 Shell with a "Dedication" 122

8 August 1992 Imitation of Life 124

10 August 1992 The Detainees of Sarajevo 127

12 August 1992 Sarajevans Blind a Sniper 130

16 August 1992 The Little Powermongers 133

18 August 1992 The Jews Leave, Sarajevo Diasappears 135

1 October 1992 To Obliterate What Has
Already Been Destroyed 138

2 October 1992 Hunger and Pigeons 141

CONTENTS

13 November 1992 The Madness, the Nausea 154

19 November 1992 Songs in Dobrinja 157

23 November 1992 Not Even the Trees Are Spared 160

2 December 1992 Close to Madness 163

5 December 1992 The Prize and the Punishment 166

19 January 1993 Nameless Horror 169

24 May 1993 To the Last Bosnian 173

15 June 1993 Worse than a Reservation 175

14 July 1993 Gentlemen and Comrades! 178

18 August 1993 The Child Hunt 181

2 February 1994 We'll Die Together and in Love 184

7 March 1994 Playing Host to Some Dubious Guests 188

4 April 1994 Back on Track 192

6 May 1994 Plundering History 197

Chronology of Events 200

Glossary of Key Persons, Places, and Organizations 206

PREFACE
BY JOSEPH BRODSKY

As America lies in its state-induced moral stupor, lots of people die violent deaths all over the place, particularly in the Balkans. When it comes to externalizing evil, few things can rival geography or, for that matter, history—that gold mine for both pundits and bandits.

What's happening now in the Balkans is very simple: It is a bloodbath. Terms such as "Serbs," "Croats," "Bosnians" mean absolutely nothing. Any other combination of vowels and consonants will amount to the same thing: killing people. Neither religious distinctions—Orthodox, Catholic, Muslim—nor ethnic ones are of any consequence. The former are forfeited with the first murder (for "Thou shalt not kill" pertains at least to any version of the Christian creed); as for the latter, all these people are what we in our parts define as Caucasian.

Evocations of history here are bare nonsense. Whenever one pulls the trigger in order to rectify history's mistake, one lies. For history makes no mistakes, since it has no purpose. One always pulls the trigger out of self-interest and quotes history to avoid responsibility or pangs of conscience. No man possesses sufficient retrospective ability to justify his deeds—murder especially—in extemporaneous categories, least of all a head of state.

Besides, the Balkan bloodshed is essentially a short-term project. Set in motion by the local heads of state, its main purpose is to keep them in power for as long as physically possible. For want of any binding issue (economic or ideological), it is prosecuted under the banner of a retroactive utopia called nationalism.

A regressive concept amounting to a flight from the multinational reality of the Balkans and the melting pot of the future Europe, nationalism boils down to settling old scores with one's neighbors. The main attraction is that it is highly absorbing (physically and mentally), that is, it takes time and provides employment for a substantial portion of the male population. For a head of state presiding over a ruined economy, an active army with its low wages is godsent: All he's got to do is provide it with an objective.

Given the Serbian troops' numerical and material superiority over their neighbors, one wonders why this objective wasn't achieved a year or two ago. The answer is that it is not in the interests of the involved heads of state.

Normally a bloodbath (especially if it is promoted to the status of war) is finite, which is to say it has a logical end at which the leader of a nation, or even a band of guerrillas, tries to arrive as speedily as possible. Then comes reconstruction, free elections, a legislative process. Now those, one imagines, are the worst nightmares of the heads of state in question, and that's what they strive to avoid through all means available.

Imagine the carnage stopped and the dust settled. What are we going to find in place of the former Yugoslavia, especially with the current men in charge still at large? A

democratic republic? A monarchy? A tyranny? None of the
above: a heap of rubble seething with hatred, topped by a
bunch of bemedaled strongmen unfit for any other job
down the heap. Hence, the slow but steady pace of carnage.
Its continuation is these men's insurance.

What should and can be done, if anything, save direct
military intervention in the region, for which our expensive military, fully deployed to defend its sexual integrity,
apparently has no stomach?

The U.S. should immediately introduce and expedite a
United Nations resolution demanding the immediate establishment of a demilitarized zone on the territory of
Bosnia and deployment of UN troops on the ground for
this purpose.

Then membership of the former Yugoslavia in the UN
should be extinguished immediately. Its flag flies outside
UN headquarters, legitimizing the Serbian leader's claim
that he is the sole guarantor of Yugoslavia's integrity and
that the bloodbath he unleashed is a struggle against
secessionists.

This membership also entitles Serbia to Yugoslavia's
substantial foreign assets (approximately $6 billion), which
by now have virtually all been spent for the prosecution of
Serbia's military campaign. Through the callousness or
neglect of the U.S. and its European allies, this was allowed
to happen.

The remaining assets, as well as the property of the
former Yugoslavia, should be immediately seized. Its em-
bassies, consular offices, airline and other administrative
representations should be closed, given up for rent, and the
proceeds should be diverted to relief programs.

Diplomatic recognition—in whatever form it currently

exists—of Serbia and Croatia should be withdrawn and not restored as long as the current heads of these states remain in power and as long as the territorial gains made in the course of hostilities by any party are not relinquished.

The current heads of these states—Slobodan Milošević of Serbia and Franjo Tudjman of Croatia, as well as the leader of the Bosnian Serbs, Radovan Karadžić—should be immediately outlawed by the UN and treated accordingly for the duration of their physical existence, particularly when hostilities cease. Which is to say that they should be denied entry into the U.S. as well as all countries with which the U.S. maintains diplomatic relations, including Switzerland.

Regardless of the outcome of the hostilities, Serbia, the unquestionable aggressor, should be obliged by UN resolution to carry the full burden of reparations.

Now, this is not much to ask from our reasonably expensive State Department. Because this would be just, it can be done unilaterally by the U.S. Justice doesn't need a consensus; it's the other way around.

The main thing for the West and for the U.S. in particular is not to go by the moronic agenda set forth by the thugs in Belgrade or Zagreb, the way the Vance-Owen team did: We should impose our own upon them. For that, of course, we ought to have one. The treatment of the matter by our Administration, while politically expedient, is ethically scandalous. People in Bosnia are digging what they now call "Clinton graves." The man deserves this; our country doesn't.

An ethical man doesn't need a consensus of his allies in order to act against something he finds reprehensible. And this is still theoretically an ethical country, judging at least by the verdict in the Federal case of Rodney King's beating.

What is taking place in the Balkans is much worse than the contents of the King tape and it takes place daily. It is called murder, and it comes to you live. Failing to have our own agenda, failing to respond to the Balkan carnage either aggressively or imaginatively, we at least shouldn't allow our pundits to obscure the sight of human blood with their well-paid verbiage. When it comes to murder, it is better to feel ashamed and impotent than informed.

In any case, we should bear in mind that all this needn't have happened. That once it began, it could have been stopped. The fact that it hasn't been stopped means that its continuation is to somebody's advantage.

We may ask, to whose? After all, ethical as we are, we are also a country of the bottom line. If somebody who can stop a bloodbath doesn't do it, it means that he profits from it. I suggest three names: Milošević, Karadžić, Tudjman. You are free to make your own list. You are also welcome to ponder whether the notion that this is an ethical country is a lie.

August 1993

INTRODUCTION
BY ROBERT JAY LIFTON

This is not a war. This is a horror that has no name. It is a black hole in the spectrum of all reasoned thought.

Everything the future may bring is already within us . . . in the strength to persevere, the will to survive. . . . [H]ere, no one lies to anyone . . . so there is hope.

—Zlatko Dizdarević

Genocide, by definition, is an ethical scandal. But the added scandal of Bosnia is the whole world's viewing genocide and doing no more than pretending to combat it. The official world organization, the United Nations, has been made into an agency of compliance—even, at times, of overseeing the killing.

Raphael Lempkin, the legal scholar, coined the word "genocide" to illuminate some of the darkest expressions of human behavior: the systematic destruction of a people or of an ethnic or religious group. He wished to make this "old practice in its modern development" a more visible and recognizable international crime. Having lost most of his own family in the Holocaust, he wanted to create new universal standards for recognizing, interrupting, and punishing this "old practice."

But Lempkin could not have anticipated the radical expansion of world media to the point of actually transmitting genocide in progress to our homes, of propelling it into our direct vision, hearing, and feeling. Only after they were inundated by such televised images was the specter of genocide in Bosnia raised for Americans. (The first request I received to comment on events there came from a division of the *The New York Times* concerned not with international relations or issues of war and peace, but with television and its impact on society.) For our television sets, and then our print media, were conveying an all-too-familiar picture of mass killing: of emaciated men in camps, mounting testimonies of the slaughter of civilians, and an added dimension of the systematic rape of women—all carried out under a clearly articulated policy of "ethnic cleansing."

Have the Bosnian Serbs grasped the extent to which the genocide they are committing has been beamed around the world? Their ability to block out that realization—or dismiss it as inconsequential—is surely enhanced by the absence of any significant world opposition to the genocide. Absence of opposition, that is, contributes greatly to the psychic numbing, the diminished capacity or inclination to feel, required by all perpetrators of genocide. So that, even as the Serbian Nationalist leaders and militiamen separate themselves psychologically from their own actions, the rest of us are brought closer to those same actions. When that happens, we find ourselves, in our associations and memories, back with the Nazis.

Yet as much as those associations increase our involvement in Bosnia, that involvement still turns out to be insufficient. The sequence goes something like this: as we register in our minds the media images of brutality and killing, our empathy for victims (efforts to imagine what they are experiencing) extends to strong sympathy and even periodic identification with them (putting ourselves in their place and becoming them). We are particularly shocked by the extent of the rape—little girls, young women, old women—mixed in with killing and with arrangements for the most extreme humiliation. Our reaction includes acute discomfort, anger, and rage toward perpetrators; feelings of shame at what is being done to people by fellow human beings; and guilt at not doing something ourselves to stop the process and instead going on with our personal pleasures and daily routines in the face of these horrors inhabiting our living rooms.

As these feelings cause us only frustration and pain, we find ourselves struggling to get rid of them. So we switch channels, or turn off our TV sets, and do what we can to call forth our own psychic numbing. We feel a little better, but we cannot quite free ourselves from some of those nagging images. We are then likely to join a general chorus of ostensibly well-meaning voices insisting that, though things are indeed terrible in Bosnia, it is all very complicated, a matter of the complicity of "all parties," derived from the "ancient hatreds" that have always characterized the endless convolutions in "the Balkans."

Are we inwardly convinced by such rote historical judgments, so convenient for justifying our own immobilization? Not entirely. Still affected by retained images of murder and suffering, we cannot wholly escape feelings of self-contempt. But we carry on. This dishonorable psychological equilibrium keeps us—and the genocide—going. We maintain the mind-set and existential state of immobilized bystanders, much like those who do nothing when an innocent person is assaulted and lies dying. More to the point, we are the "good Germans" who turn the other way while Jewish acquaintances or colleagues are rounded up and killed.

Many of those good Germans could claim that they did not understand what was being done to the Jews, that the Nazis had kept them from knowledge of the larger murderous project. The claims tended to be self-serving, as there were many degrees of knowledge and half-knowledge, along with what has been called a will not to know. But it is true that full knowledge of the genocide was interfered with by systematic efforts on the part of the Nazis to hide their actions. In the case of the Bosnian Serbs, however, virtually nothing is hidden from us—not the details of the killings and rapes, nor the overall pursuit of ethnic cleansing. We belong to a new category in our relation to genocide, that of informed bystanders.

Here and there, Americans have been able to transmute their psychological confusion into a constructive stand for multilateral intervention in Bosnia. Indeed, emotions of the kind I have described—but with still greater components of anger and frustration—have contributed to the resignation of four State Department officials concerned with American policy in the former Yugoslavia. Genuine moral and political leadership could have helped large numbers of people to undergo that transformation from immobilizing fragmentary awareness to the kind of integrated awareness that enables one to join in a shared effort to stop the genocide. Instead, our inaction has become a form of immoral action. We have betrayed both the Bosnians and our own more decent and responsible selves. More than that, in tolerating—and periodically facilitating—visible genocide, we have to a degree entered into a genocidal mentality.

A genocidal mentality consists of participation in, advocacy of, or support of policies and actions aimed at the annihilation of entire human populations. While there have been all too many genocides over the past few decades in various parts of the world—in East Asia, Africa, the Indian subcontinent, and South America—the Nazis have provided us with our twentieth-century model. In studying Nazi doctors, I came to observe a psychological and historical sequence that seems to occur in virtually all expressions of genocide. There is, first, a collective sense of historical trauma, of a wound to the bodies and psyches of one's people, to the point of demoralization and perceived "illness." In the case of Germany, there was the overwhelmingly painful defeat in World War I, itself following upon profound prior confusions surrounding modernization and national unification. There is next the emergence of an ideology of revitalization and cure: the Nazi promise to make Germans and Germany strong and "healthy" again, a promise of individual, national. and ethnic renewal. At some point—and this is the crucial step—the ideology becomes genocidal, or at least calls into action latent genocidal impulses in the movement. The example here was what I call the Nazi biomedical vision: that of excising the deadly Jewish "infection" in order to bring about recovery and new strength to the Nordic race. Intellectuals and professionals provide the ideological rationale for killing, along with the technology: Nazi doctors were a sinister case in point.

We can then speak of "killing professionals" and "professional killers," both groups driven by ideology but also having the potential for adding an array of self-aggrandizing and psychopathic tendencies. A threshold is crossed, sometimes haphazardly, after which there is no turning back from genocide: the Nazis crossed theirs sometime during the first half of 1941. Just how that happened is still not fully understood, but historians now give some importance to such factors as the problem of feeding and otherwise coping with the large numbers of Jews rounded up in ghettos, and perceptions on the part of Nazi officials, in their back-and-forth communications with the leadership, of "what the Führer wanted."

Even if the scale of killing is minuscule compared with that of the Nazis, and the technology less efficient, Serbian behavior is no less genocidal. And although the Serbs have not been alone in applying principles of ethnic cleansing to areas of the former Yugoslavia, they have been the predominant perpetrators of genocide. Their pattern, moreover, follows the same general sequence as that of the Nazis. Their historical pain and grievance derive from frustrated national aims following the death of one-half the adult male population in World War I, and occupation and massacre during World War II. In the latter case, the victimizers were not only the Germans but Croatian fascists, and to some extent Bosnian Muslims as well. And under Titoist communism, nationalist sentiments could serve as a locus of resistance. But these historical memories have been systematically manipulated, as have much older ones dating back to the Turkish conquest of the fourteenth century. The lethal puppeteers often turn out to be former communist leaders suddenly turned fierce nationalists, or lawless militiamen and soldiers of fortune who thrive on violence. Such leaders have put together haphazard but powerful ideological elements that stress, above all, Serbian ethnic virtue as opposed to Bosnian and Croatian perfidy. Territorial aggression is sometimes joined to a confused and contradictory vision of a "greater Serbia" that has some of the millenarian spirit of the "thousand-year Reich." In any such national or ethnic vision, there is a claimed "higher purpose" having to do with the glory—the immortalization—of one's own people. But to achieve that purpose, one must select suitable victims to bear the death taint; one kills in order to destroy death.

As with Nazi ideology, much of the concept and policy of ethnic cleansing was worked out and articulated by professionals and intellectuals, in the Serbian case by members of the Academy of Sciences. The Serbian crossing of the genocidal threshold was also apparently the result of mutual influence between nationalist leaders in Belgrade and sub-leaders, political and military, among Bosnian Serbs. Each has provided its share of both professional killers and killing professionals.

Serbian excesses occur at a time of a worldwide impulse toward ethnic purification, much of it taking on a fundamentalist character. That ethnic ferocity becomes a refuge not only from post-communist and post-cold war confusion, but also from the radical decline in the overall legitimacy of the state. Governments throughout the world are increasingly seen as corrupt, destructive, and oppressive entities, or at best, as distant, ineffectual, and unresponsive to human needs. Governments can no longer protect people from the high-technology weaponry of enemies or from large-scale environmental disasters, such as Chernobyl, whose effects are in no way contained by national borders. Ethnic ties, in contrast, offer close, organic relationships, something on the order of an expanded biological attachment. Such ties are necessary to all of us, and can offer vital forms of connectedness and self-definition. But in the absence of a larger human principle, they can be readily exploited and pressed in the direction of totalism—of all-or-none polarizations between "us" and "them"—as has been true of the Nazi and Serbian examples.

But neither fanatic ethnic nationalism nor psychopathic violence is required for a genocidal mentality. One need only consider the extent to which another kind of genocidal project, that related to nuclear weapons, can claim the support of ordinary, essentially decent people. Quite appropriately, there took place in Sarajevo on August 6, 1993, a day of commemoration of the forty-eighth anniversary of the atomic bombing of Hiroshima. The announcement spoke of the two cities as being "united in the fellowship of suffering." The post-Hiroshima genocidal mentality, most intense in the United States and the Soviet Union over the course of the cold war, stemmed largely from what must be termed a perverse reaction to Hiroshima. In America, after a period of post-bomb soul-searching and expressions of fear for the human future, a decision was made to embrace the very source of that terror. The evolving ideology of nuclearism, which soon extended to the Soviet Union, included extreme dependency on the weapons, and attraction to their ultimate power to the point of near-worship. The "deterrence" policy emerging from that ideology always included a willingness to use the weapons under certain conditions, thereby creating a genocidal threshold waiting to be crossed. As supporters of such policies, millions of ordinary people were linked to a genocidal mentality. The process could be greatly enhanced by placing the weapons in a realm of fascinating technology, thereby producing the kind of psychic numbing that protects one from feeling what goes on at the other end.

In the past, when genocide was being projected and carried out, the policy has been to make it known only to ideologically "advanced" supporters of the project and to the required technicians and foot soldiers. For the Nazis, that elite group included high leadership, specific SS divisions, and certain medical units. Similarly, in regard to the draconian nuclear scenarios put forward by the United States and the Soviet Union, full details have been available only to the privileged nuclear priesthood and their higher governmental authorities. After a genocide has been completed, the victimizers tend to deny, either partially or completely, what they have done. Such denial on the part of Nazis and neo-Nazis is well known, and becomes all the more pernicious by making contact with ordinary people's psychological resistance to the grotesque and unacceptable truths of the Holocaust. Less known is the systematic cover-up of the Turkish genocide of Armenians—which Serbian genocide more closely resembles—conducted mainly in 1915. The present Turkish government has spent huge sums of money in hiring American advertising firms as well as corruptible or naive academics, to endorse that denial.

The Turkish genocide, however, was quite real to Hitler himself: he in fact invoked it to create momentum for his own mass killing. In briefing his SS generals for their annihilation of the Polish Intelligencia—a prefiguring of the genocide of Jews—Hitler asked his infamous rhetorical question: "Who still talks nowadays of the extermination of the Armenians?" Here Hitler was drawing upon the world's failure to interrupt a previous genocide—or even to attend to it—as a source of inspiration for moving toward crossing his own genocidal threshold. Precisely that kind of inspiration from Serbian genocide could be experienced by demagogic leaders everywhere, most immediately by those in other parts of Eastern Europe, dangerously so in countries derived from the former Soviet Union.

But the mass media have made it almost impossible to keep any genocide secret for very long. Today, any image from any culture, present or past, can be made available, almost instantaneously, virtually everywhere. Oppressors in general find it harder to keep secrets, as they discovered when confronted with the democracy movements during the late eighties and early nineties in Central and Eastern Europe, China, and South Africa.

To be sure, the media can cut both ways. During the Vietnam War, the televised killings and burnings of villages could be rendered for many an entertainment, another John Wayne film. But once the viewer began to question the war, began to form a concept of American atrocities, every televised suggestion of killing became a further stimulus to troubling doubt and passionate opposition. It was not so much the critical reports of journalists that fueled American opposition—these were in fact relatively few, and for the most part came quite late in the war—as the actual images of death and suffering to which Americans could have access.

The American military absorbed this lesson in its policies during the Gulf War. It imposed extraordinary censorship to make sure that nothing ugly, like death, especially of civilians, would be made visible. Contributing to this covering over of death was the technological distancing of the air war and the particular American fascination with high-tech bombing, catered to by the media by means of myriad charts and an endless parade of retired generals and admirals for "expert" technical analysis. Yet CNN's twenty-four-hour coverage nonetheless permitted certain sights and sounds of war to make their way into living rooms in America and throughout the world. And subsequent media reports have contributed to a retrospective exposure of the dimensions of killing in the Gulf War. It would seem that no nation or violent group can any longer prevent its large-scale killing from becoming a world event.

Serbian genocide has been a world event almost from its beginnings, but until now we have lacked detailed reports from where the killing has been taking place. Zlatko Dizdarević, in this compelling and indispensable book, tells us about genocide from the inside. We gain knowledge that television could never convey about what we have been allowing to happen to people in a city called Sarajevo, a city notable for its general tolerance and its ethnic and religious mixture. Dizdarević does not speak for "Muslims," "Croats," or "Serbs," but on behalf of his fellow human beings. He calls us to a recognition of our species mentality, of a recognition that whatever our ethnic and religious attachments, we are capable of combining these with, and subsuming them to, our membership in humankind.

It is too late to reverse our betrayals, but never too late to change course. That would mean remobilizing our world organization, and ourselves in serving it, and empowering it to make use of its own charter to intervene to stop the killing and establish conditions for democratic behavior and sustained peace. Such action would begin to respond in kind to the extraordinary humanity of the people Diz-darević describes, and would also permit a tiny ray of light to enter this dark night of our own souls.

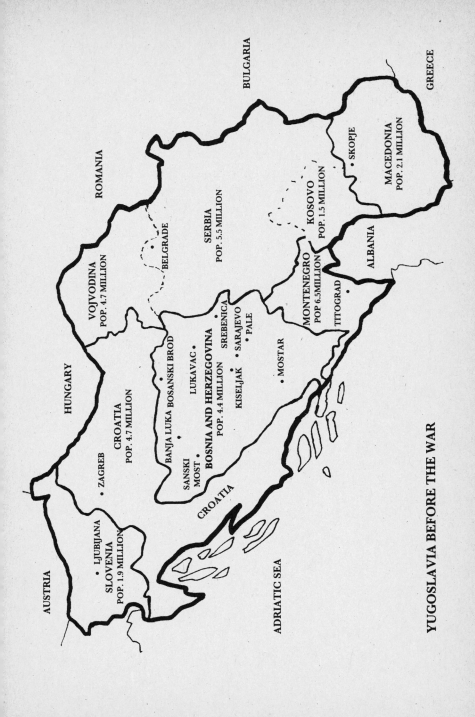

AUSTRIA

HUNGARY

ROMANIA

BULGARIA

GREECE

SLOVENIA
POP. 1.9 MILLION
• LJUBJANA

CROATIA
POP. 4.7 MILLION
• ZAGREB

VOJVODINA
POP. 4.7 MILLION

• BELGRADE

SERBIA
POP. 5.5 MILLION

BANJA LUKA BOSANSKI BROD
LUKAVAC •
SANSKI
MOST •
BOSNIA AND HERZEGOVINA
POP. 4.4 MILLION
SREBENICA •
KISELJAK • SARAJEVO
• PALE
• MOSTAR

CROATIA

KOSOVO
POP. 1.5 MILLION

MACEDONIA
POP. 2.1 MILLION
• SKOPJE

ALBANIA

MONTENEGRO
POP. 6.5 MILLION
• TITOGRAD

ADRIATIC SEA

YUGOSLAVIA BEFORE THE WAR

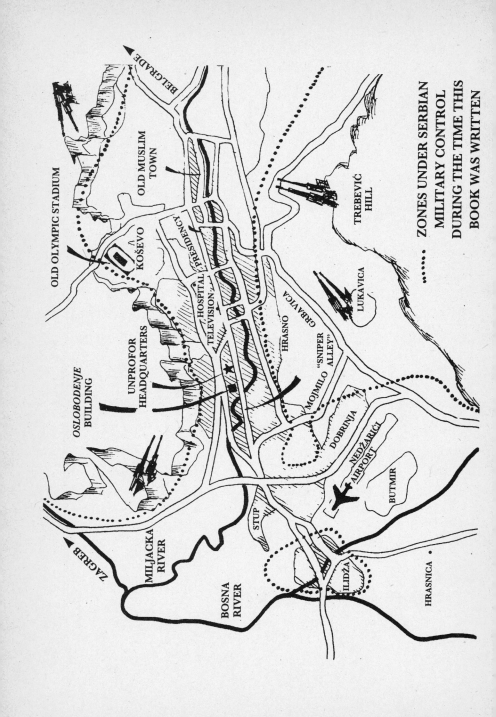

ZONES UNDER SERBIAN
MILITARY CONTROL
DURING THE TIME THIS
BOOK WAS WRITTEN

THE ZONES OF CONFLICT IN THE FORMER YUGOSLAVIA DURING THE TIME THIS BOOK WAS WRITTEN

☐ Occupied by the Serbian nationalist forces

☐ Croatian Control

☐ Muslim Control

☐ Croatian and Muslim Control

☐ Zones protected by the UNPROFOR

SARAJEVO

A WAR JOURNAL

MADNESS AGAINST REASON:
A NOTE TO
THE AMERICAN READER

From the very beginning of the present war in what used to be Yugoslavia, and particularly in Bosnia-Herzegovina, one has heard this theory: "It's an outbreak of sheer madness, and no one knows what it's all about . . . It is a war in which everyone fights everyone else, and you can't make sense out of it." However, those who know even a little about Yugoslavia before the war, and about the events that led to the war, understand that this is not the case. For them, I will briefly describe the sad fate of Bosnia-Herzegovina, and of Sarajevo.

The simple fact is that a conglomerate of fanatical nationalists, political careerists, and malcontents—for the most part, people who never felt comfortable with law, order, and democracy—realized they could launch violent aggression without fear of reprisal from the outside world, since that outside world's "priorities" would keep it from intervening. They were not mistaken. By violence, by crimes, by open military aggression, genocide, and ethnic purification of entire territories, they have managed to change the geographical and ethnic map of Bosnia-

Herzegovina. They have violated fundamental principles concerning human rights, international borders, military intervention, the occupation of sovereign states, and so forth. In Sarajevo, a city under siege for more than fifteen months, old people, women, and children continue to be killed by long-range artillery fire. A six-hundred-year-old city has been destroyed. The outside world watches without reacting beyond issuing cynical statements to the effect that this is a "civil war" whose "combatants cannot be given any aid."

But what is happening in Bosnia-Herzegovina is *not* a civil war—even though it may now, after all that has occurred, manifest some characteristics of one. This state, admitted to the United Nations and officially recognized by a large number of countries, has become a victim of aggression from the outside. The aggressors are Serbia and Montenegro, who are reinforced by extremist nationalist forces operating within Bosnia-Herzegovina, and they are using military resources left over or taken by them from the former Yugoslav Army.

It began in 1987 in Belgrade with the rise to power of an extremist regime whose leader, Slobodan Milošević, an orthodox Communist, was opposed to any structural modification of the Yugoslav federation proposed by the current moderate political opinion. The establishment of this authoritarian and centralized regime in Belgrade strengthened the desire of Slovenia and Croatia to gain their independence from Belgrade, and with the help of the European Community they managed to do so. The Republic of Bosnia-Herzegovina followed their example; most of its people did not want to remain under the rule of Slobodan Milošević's Belgrade and its "new Yugoslavia."

The citizens of Bosnia-Herzegovina felt that a Yugoslavia without all its former republics, without Slovenia and Croatia, would no longer be Yugoslavia.

The international community formally authorized Bosnia-Herzegovina to proclaim its independence, on condition that there would be a referendum in which the inhabitants would be asked whether they wanted a sovereign republic or whether they wanted to remain part of the new, truncated Yugoslavia. The results of this referendum, which was supervised by observers from all over the world, were quite unequivocal: more than sixty percent of the voters preferred independence. Following the examples of Slovenia and Croatia, Bosnia-Herzegovina proclaimed itself a sovereign republic in October 1991 and passed a referendum for independence in February 1992. It was later admitted to the United Nations as well as to all important international organizations and institutions. Only the Belgrade regime refused to accept this solution, and this refusal led to the war.

After its unsuccessful military intervention in Slovenia had been halted, the old Yugoslav Army first attacked Croatia, then Bosnia-Herzegovina. In the latter, it first armed all the extremists who showed themselves willing to fight for Belgrade's objectives. Those objectives had been clearly defined several years earlier in a document composed by members of the Serbian Academy of Sciences in Belgrade. The essential message of this text is contained in one of its most simple sentences: "Every square meter of Yugoslavia inhabited by at least one Serb shall be part of the state of Serbia." The ideological father of this movement, the writer Dobrica Ćosić, who subsequently became President of the non-recognized state of Yugoslavia, told the leader of Bosnia-Herzegovina's Serb extremists, Rado-van Karadžić, at the very beginning of the war: "In Bosnia, you must do everything to make what seemed impossible yesterday, possible today. . . ."

Alas, that is exactly what they have done. After an unprecedented media blitz of aggressive hate propaganda on behalf of "all that is Serb," an equally unprecedented crime wave washed over Bosnia-Herzegovina. Its purpose was to conquer as much territory as possible, to expel all non-Serbs and opponents of the Milošević regime, and, finally, to incorporate these conquered territories into the state of Serbia. In ten months of war, almost two hundred thousand civilians have died in Bosnia-Herzegovina, and two million inhabitants have been forced out of their homes. Sarajevo, a city of some six hundred thousand, has been completely surrounded. It is impossible to enter or to leave the city, and electricity and water supplies have been interrupted. The city is being shelled every day; ten thousand people have been killed, two thousand of them children. More than fifty thousand people have been injured. Almost all of these victims have been civilians. There really is no "war" in Sarajevo, merely a continuous bombardment of the city from the surrounding hills and their Serb gun emplacements, armed with artillery given to the aggressors by the old Yugoslav army.

Nevertheless, the war in Bosnia-Herzegovina is not a war between nationalities. Despite the siege, Sarajevo is still the home of more than eighty thousand Serbs and thirty thousand Croats who do not want to leave their city, their homes, and their friends. More than forty percent of the city's marriages are mixed. Before the war, no one in Sarajevo made much of ethnic or religious allegiances. *That* is why the aggressors wish to destroy this city: it reveals the fascist nature of the claim that there is no longer a place for mixed communities in Bosnia-Herzegovina. Unfortunately, the world of international politics has, through a combination of indifference on the one hand and organized support for the nationalists on the other, reinforced the siege of Sarajevo and the genocide perpetrated here.

The pieces collected in this book, most of which were written during the first months of the siege, and all of which were written in spontaneous reaction to what was happening, don't deal directly with the political games played by the international community. We Sarajevans have no overview of those. These pieces are an attempt to tell what is happening to ordinary people in a city that refuses to die, to people who find it incredible that such events can take place in plain view of the world, under the eyes of those who claim to respect justice, order, law, and liberty. Hence, they may convey a single message; they show that Dobrica Ćosić, regrettably, has been vindicated: everything that seemed impossible yesterday—the demolition of a civilized, cosmopolitan European city with old cultures and traditions—has become entirely possible today. In addition, these texts may increase awareness that Sarajevo's story is not unique—many other towns like it lie along the road of the madmen who have ruined it. As a Sarajevan who has seen and lived through these events, I am compelled to broadcast a warning: there are sick people in this world who now understand that they are dealing with a public that, when it comes to international politics, is egotistical, incompetent, and unrealistic. We are witnessing a renascence of Nazism and Fascism, and no one is willing to call a halt to it. We are witnessing the abolition of all recognized human values.

As for us Sarajevans, we have to put our trust in ourselves. We are proud of what once was our city of friends. One day, we—those of us who will survive—will have the honor of telling our children that we were Sarajevans. Personally, I consider it a duty to remain in my city until the end, and to go on writing about it as long as I am able.

25 April 1992

BOSNIAN ROULETTE

Today news we had feared for two weeks reached the offices of *Oslobodenje*: our colleague in Zvornik, Kjašif Smajlović, can no longer be counted among the missing. Sadly, his assassination has been confirmed. It is now clear that he was treacherously murdered on the ninth of April, on the doorstep of *Oslobodenje*'s Zvornik office, when Serb territorials and their various collaborators "liberated" Zvornik. Friends who buried Kjašif tell us he had gone to the office to file his report on how the attackers began their reign of terror. He was dragged out, feet first, and calmly executed on the sidewalk.

Among the hundreds, even thousands, of assassinations perpetrated in "liberated" Bosnia-Herzegovina, a journalist's death may seem just as tragic as any other. There is, however, a slight difference that, today in particular, ought to be noted. The outrages committed in Bosnia-Herzegovina and Sarajevo, whether assassinations or other crimes, confirm a statement made recently on television by one of our journalists who was once our special correspondent in Lebanon: Any comparison between our present situation and that of Lebanon ten years ago can only be an insult to the Lebanese. Not one journalist was killed there solely because he was a journalist and wanted to report to his office what he had seen with his own eyes. In Lebanon, no one deliberately fired at a Red Cross vehicle, and no physician who tried to help a wounded person was ever killed. And no one in Lebanon kidnapped three buses with two hundred children who were trying, under the auspices of the Children's Embassy organization, to escape from a bleeding city ravaged by army tanks and artillery.

All of this, however, has happened in Sarajevo over the last thirty hours. We have learned that one of our friends has been viciously murdered, simply because he was our colleague. A paramedic was killed while trying to get across town to help someone whose life depended on his care. Meanwhile, busloads of children and the doctors accompanying them were being held as bargaining chips in negotiations for the release of seven terrorists from Ilidža. In the end, the exchange took place. It has come to seem quite normal and natural, this simultaneous release of a group of panic-stricken children who were trying to escape from hell, and seven criminals who have been showering mortar shells on those same children and their parents. . . .

Today it was warm and sunny in Sarajevo. In the center of the city, on the principal artery, there were moments when you were reminded of the good old days. The occasional shots fired from a distance couldn't spoil the small daily pleasures of a spring walk. On the other hand, those parts of the city that have had no electricity, water, or bread for three days, and which one cannot leave because *chetniks**, terrorists, and tanks hold them captive, can thank

---

*Serbian nationalists in World War II allied with the Nazis and the name given to Serbian nationalist forces in Bosnia.

their lucky stars they still exist. This may be the intention of those who guard their "liberty." But there are still some people who don't believe in that kind of "liberty," not even at the price of their heads. They roll up their trousers and ford the Željeznica river, trying to come within reach of the city. Then it is up to those who control that passage from the neighboring hills to decide, at random, whom they'll let pass and whom they'll shoot: Bosnian roulette in the spring sunshine.

Well-informed people claim that long military columns have been leaving Sarajevo since yesterday evening. There are rumors that the Yugoslav National Army is definitely withdrawing. But at the moment, it is more important to decide what to do about those who will remain—those capable of firing at ambulances, kidnapping children, and dragging journalists out of their offices to assassinate them in the street.

Indeed, we should not be insulting the Lebanese.

WHEN LIBERATORS OCCUPY TRUTH

The war in Bosnia-Herzegovina is what it is—pitiless, cruel, and savage. Very often it lacks rational objectives, except for a fundamental and general one: conquering as much territory as possible to be annexed to the new state on the other side of the river Drina. But in addition to what one might expect from any armed conflict in the world, this Bosnian inferno imprints its particular horrors on all our memories. These consist of acts of savagery and barbarity that have long been catalogued and classified in the multitude of international documents, conventions, and declarations the world uses to protect itself against what it has recognized as unmitigated evil. One of the crimes of this genre—the attempt to seize radio, television, and telecommunications stations by armed force—is taking place even as I write. On Thursday evening, the army that still calls itself the Yugoslav People's Army, aided by Serbian terrorists dragged in from Krajina, mounted an operation against the television relay station on Mount Vlašić, above Travnik. Its obvious intention was to do what already has been done to more than half the relay stations in Bosnia-

Herzegovina: seize the station, drive away the regular TV Sarajevo staff, replace it with "liberators," and turn the antennae around to the transmitters of TV Serbia. What this amounts to is that the truth itself is "occupied." Instead of the truth of what is actually being done to our city, people will be told monstrous lies by those who have come to "liberate" us.

However, the battle for Vlašić won't prove as easy and painless as the takeover of relay stations on Mt. Kozara, Mt. Plješevica, Mt. Velež, and elsewhere. The meadows and pasturelands of Vlašić, famous until recently for tourism and for Travnik cheese, may be the proving ground for the future of the "Yugoslav" army in Bosnia-Herzegovina. Bosnian forces defending Travnik and its environs are said to be among the strongest and best organized in the whole republic. The decision to provoke them like this is yet another example of the insane strategies of Belgrade's military junta; these strategies make it only too obvious how pointless it is to negotiate with them.

If the battle over the television relays at Vlašić manages to disturb the cool and reasonable mind of Europe; it will lead to the unavoidable, frightening question: does the ultimatum of the "Yugoslav" army to a handful of technicians—its demand that they abandon the station— mean that the army is set on launching a well-organized, well-armed operation? Is this army consciously entering a difficult battle at Vlašić with the intention of going further? Or is it merely another expression of the primitive and barbaric urge to unleash violence against everything in this region which the rest of the world regards as inviolable? It's all right to shoot paramedics, kidnap children, "arrest" entire villages, steal international humanitarian aid supplies; now it's even all right to turn around television transmitters.

No doubt today and tomorrow, the audience watching the programs from those transmitters will learn that the army has survived a treacherous attack by Croatian Defense Forces (HOS) and Green Berets (Muslims) on Vlašić, and that it was "compelled to respond forcefully with all the means at its disposal." And after that, neither European observers nor the UN Protection Force will be allowed to set foot in the area for weeks, nor in any other part of Bosnia-Herzegovina where there has been a "forceful response to provocations" and extermination of "aggressors" as first practiced in Croatia—where the bodies of such aggressors were loaded into refrigerated trucks and taken away, only to have every trace of them lost. But, nonetheless, the "liberators" forget one incontrovertible fact: truth does not reside in a transmitter.

DIRTY POLITICS

In Sarajevo a three-year-old girl playing outside her home is hit by a sniper's bullet. Her horrified father carries her to the hospital. Bleeding, she hovers between life and death. Only after her father, a big hulk of a man, has found a doctor to care for her does he allow himself to burst into tears. The television camera records his words. These words, every one of them, belong in an anthology of humanism, helplessness, and forgiveness at its most extreme—not so much forgiving the criminal who shot a three-year-old child, as forgiving the wild beasts for *being* wild beasts, for being debased by an evil that destroys every human impulse. Two of his sentences accompany thoughts that will linger long past today or tomorrow. The first comes when the stricken father invites the unknown assassin to *have a cup of coffee with him so that he can tell him, like a human being, what has brought him to do such a thing.* Then he says, aware that this question may not elicit any *human response*: "One day her tears will catch up with him. . . . "

There is absolutely nothing to be done for this nation. It will never attain justice and happiness if it cannot bring itself to recognize an executioner as an executioner, a murderer as a murderer, a criminal as a criminal. If the most barbaric act imaginable in this war, a sniper shooting at a three-year-old girl playing in front of her own home, elicits only an invitation to a cup of coffee and hope for forgiveness, then Bosnia-Herzegovina doesn't stand much chance to survive.

When Marrack Goulding, that civilized American, arrived here in his capacity as a high-ranking UN official, and after seeing all that has happened here, after hearing what is going on in Mostar, being subjected to ill-treatment by the orthodox *chetniks* of Pale, and having been shot at by a sniper while examining the damage suffered by the old town of Baščaršija—when after all that he declared that "all sides are equally responsible," we had to realize at last that this latest maneuver was no more than a matter of dirty politics; it had nothing to do with any reality apparent to the naked eye. Here no one knows, as yet, the kind of political games he and his superiors are playing—the horrendous nature of those deals, the promises made to the Germans, and vice versa. In this game, Milošević and Bosnia are merely pawns, but pawns of whom? When the father of a small girl shot by a sniper, devastated by grief, invites the assassin to a cup of coffee in order to convey his message to him, then the only thing left for us is to remember the Biblical appeal, "Forgive them, for they know not what they do." But let us not be naive; the problem here is that they know very well what they're doing. Just as Mr. Goulding knows that they know.

What then can give us hope for the future? Forgiveness? Closing our eyes to the bullets fired by criminals who take pleasure in murdering children? Waiting for the outcome of negotiations between Karadžić and Boras, who are said to be approaching an agreement on the peaceful division of Bosnia-Herzegovina? In whose name, with what right, and for whose benefit? Who are these two gentlemen anyway? One is a terrorist, an international criminal by every criterion established by Interpol. The other, a little old man who thinks his dirty little treason will buy him the pardon of history. To negotiate with the ringleader of snipers who shoot at children and with the leaders of criminal gangs who are destroying Mostar and Sarajevo is a crime in itself. To put it bluntly: we will never find our way out of this madness in a madhouse where both the patients and the therapists are collaborating against sanity. The Karadžić-Boras agreement might be worth something only if the matter of snipers shooting at a three-year-old *could* be settled over a cup of coffee and a piece of *rahat-loukoum*.* Since this can never be so, what remains is that second statement, in which the unfortunate father of the even more unfortunate child speaks the absolute truth: "Her tears will catch up with him." How so? Because those tears will come from another world, a normal world in which pain and suffering have a meaning—a meaning that cannot be obliterated by the meaningless acts of madmen, criminals, terrorists, and political pickpockets.

*Turkish delight.

10 May 1992

TO LEAVE OR TO STAY

In Sarajevo, a city where a steady rain of mortar shells falls from the sky, there are three morning indicators that let you gauge what the first few hours of the day will be like. First, obviously, are the sounds of war. If they're limited to a few machine-gun bursts and their echoes from the surrounding mountains, punctuated by a few explosions and detonations, that means business as usual. The Old Town will suffer a little more damage, a few people will need an ambulance, but the sum of suffering won't rise above what one has grown accustomed to.

The second indicator is the image of the broadcasting building's surroundings, projected onto television screens from a camera installed on the roof of the building. Hour by hour this building is gradually being transformed into a gigantic concrete sieve. The image transmitted by the camera covers less than a mile of street on either side of the building. If more than five people cross this area every minute or two, it is a good sign, and every car that flashes from one side of the screen to the other indicates a good morning too.

The third indicator, the most important, is what you see on the street from your own window. This war can't be lost as long as mothers and wives go out to find a piece of bread, or a bunch of nettles, or, if they're really lucky, some cans of food. On their heels, children go down into the courtyards, ignoring the pleas of parents or siblings to come back inside. After that, the café crowd ventures out—local representatives of each quarter, who meet each other more warmly and pleasantly than they ever did in the old official organizations we used to have. Thus the day can begin, and it is up to the *chetniks* and other terrorists to decide what they want to do with it.

Our modest intimate exchanges in this everyday existence, when we're not busy saving our skins, revolve around stories of people who still live here, and stories of those who no longer dwell among us, for one reason or another. About those who are here, we soon learn more than we've ever known before. We unearth old stories that for years have only served to accompany an occasional nod. We identify with our own past in a new way; we realize the emptiness of some friendships, and the need to return to others which now appear in a new light. In this world consisting only of a street and with no phones or freedom of movement, you see the only thing that matters—(in)humanity. And from this perspective, we ask the questions: Who left, why, and where have they gone? Who stayed simply because he or she did not want to leave? Today you include those who haven't been able to leave in the category of those who didn't want to leave. And that is as it should be.

As for those who have left, who once were a unique part of Sarajevo, who swore by Sarajevo, who got out of Sarajevo everything they could before secretly embarking on military airplanes—or who knows what other kind of plane—they are another story, and one talked about without too many nuances. We're not talking of the turncoats who have

have fled to Pale, from where Sarajevo is being bombarded around the clock—we no longer consider them human, they are just animals. We're talking about businessmen and journalists, singers and musicians, comedians and politicians, directors and international stars. Some of them, it seems, have pangs of conscience: From time to time they try to tell us, from far away, that they aren't doing well and that they suffer because of us. Some don't tell us anything. And some have nothing to say.

From here, it is indeed difficult to judge their motivations; fear may be the most human of them. How can you blame anyone who has fled the big concentration camp Sarajevo is gradually becoming? Maybe we are tormented by the fact that many of them knew what was about to happen, but left without warning their friends, especially their friends with young children. But when the time comes, everything will be returned to its original place.

While waiting for that time, we enjoy the mornings when the shooting is sporadic, when wives and mothers quietly emerge to continue their search for the means to go on living. We enjoy seeing five cars and a dozen people per minute on our television screens. The gathering of the local community at the café should conclude without casualties, in spite of a dozen or so shots from the usual snipers who compel us to change chairs from time to time.

So those who have left shouldn't worry that we've forgotten them. We think and talk about them a great deal. We are delighted that they are doing well. When we have liberated Sarajevo, we'll live together again, we'll know one another, I know what kind of people we are. . . .

BAD NEWS

Yesterday the fears of Sarajevans were confirmed. A new cease-fire agreement was signed here, and in New York the gentlemen of the Security Council adopted yet another resolution concerning us. It has been given a new number, but it looks, once again, like no more than a finger pointing lamely to admonish Serbia and the Army.

On this subject, a British diplomat has made two amusing remarks. *Primo*: "Those who ignore the resolutions of the UN do so at their own risk." *Secundo*: "It is difficult to do anything here, since it is an 'ethnic conflict.'"

The net result has been a new ferocious attack launched on our city last night. From the *Oslobodenje* tower I saw thousands of tracer bullets rain down on Sarajevo. According to the Englishman's statements, made in New York, the bullets that come to rest in our apartments and on our roofs can distinguish who is who in this "ethnic conflict."

Early this morning from the window of our editorial office, we watched the departure of a long convoy of UN Protection Force trucks. Silently—not to say bowing their heads in shame—they left in their armored vehicles and white trucks. It had taken them all night to organize this convoy in front of the building they had inhabited and affectionately nicknamed "Rainbow Hotel." They left at dawn. It was the coup de grâce to all our hopes, our hospitality, our fears for their lives. They had represented a psychological guarantee for our safety. We haven't felt as miserable, betrayed, and abandoned for a long time as we did when this file of white vehicles pulled away from the site of our suffering.

The moment they left, the killers stationed on the surrounding hills opened fire on the city. This was their way of expressing their feelings about the departure of the Blue Helmets. Their psychological victory obviously pleased them to no end.

We felt frustrated, and abandoned to our grief, but out of it arose this recognition: It is better for us to be left alone, since foreigners are clearly powerless in the face of what is happening here. The great illusion has been dispelled. Now we know that everyone has to find their own way, and fight for their life, alone. Only through your strength will you survive, and no one owes any gratitude elsewhere.

As of today, this city begins to die in a new way, the hardest of all: most of its districts no longer have water or electricity. Those in the know are saying that we haven't seen anything yet. In the hospitals, conditions for normal surgery and blood transfusions have become impossible.

This morning a man told me, "From my window I saw a heartrending scene. My neighbor was killed by a sniper bullet. For several days we tried in vain to take his body to a cemetery. Finally, we had to bury him in front of a building. His friends made a coffin out of a kitchen table and a wooden sign. They managed to bury him, under sniper fire. . . ."

Do the gentlemen in New York know that this is happening, despite their resolutions, and after the signing of the cease-fire agreement? Do they know that they're being told lies? But it isn't over yet. We'll go on. And if we get no more resolutions or cease-fire agreements for the next couple of days, we'll be better off for it.

LANA'S CHILDHOOD

Today has been, so far, a calm day in Sarajevo. Calm, that is, if one considers isolated sniper fire and a few brief bursts from heavy or light machine guns insignificant. Nevertheless, such peaceful moments create another kind of torment. Across the ashes of the city, and past ruins we could never have imagined, drift questions that hold sleep at bay just as effectively as detonating mortar shells: What will become of us tomorrow? What will happen to this city, and this country? How will we live in what used to be Mostar or Sarajevo? What will the new life be like, assuming there is a new life?

The criminals have already destroyed half the city, perhaps a little more, perhaps a little less. What drives home the extent of destruction is the number of razed buildings that used to define the city's skyline. What is Sarajevo without the central railroad station, without Elektroprivreda, without Higijenski Zavod, without the Holiday Inn, without Valter Perić, without the old post office, without Unioninvest, without the School of Forestry, the technical lyceum, and on and on. . . . But what does all that matter, against the destroyed friendships, broken relationships, betrayals by former friends; against the total collapse of all human standards, of our previous understanding of the world and its relationships? What does a destroyed and incinerated chocolate factory or car matter, compared to a world literally annihilated under the eyes of our children, in order to imprint the labels of Serb, Muslim, and Croat forever on every verb, adjective, and noun of the language? Who will pay for this? And who will be able to forgive these children for the emotional disorders they will suffer from for the rest of their lives?

Yesterday, in the midst of the chaos of war, a small news item arrived, so small it was almost imperceptible, announcing that the school year 1991–92 is now over, and that the students' grades will be the same as they were on the first day of the war, while failing grades have been raised by one point.

My friend Boro, who with other colleagues stays around the clock at the offices of *Oslobodenje* in order to protect and produce the paper, received the news from his daughter, whom the war has prevented from finishing her first school year. On the day classes were canceled, all her grades were five out of five, and thus she finished this truncated year with perfect grades. Do you know what she asked for, timidly and in a near-whisper, to celebrate this success? "Papa—since I've done so well, could you buy me an ice cream cone?"

Boro is a man of the world, competent and successful. Before she started school, Lana could have had all the ice cream she wanted. In those days, before the destruction and the tears, Lana would have been rewarded for her grades with whatever Boro could have afforded to buy her. Today, even in her great little world, she has understood the meaning of the sights that surround her, she has assimilated the message of values circumscribed by hunger and thirst, poverty, grief, and loss. And in her great little world, that ice cream has become a dream that can only be hoped for.

Those who have reduced Lana's dreams to an ice cream cone, and her years to come to a never-ending, subconscious fear of mortar shells that breed hunger, thirst, and suffering—do they believe they'll be forgiven and forgotten? Do they really believe they can escape from children who will know, tomorrow and the day after, the reasons for what happened to them, and who was responsible for it? There is no escape. This is clear to us, to the children, and to them.

18 May 1992

LIFE SUSPENDED BY A THREAD

A bizarre calm reigns. In a city this size the streets are deserted. There is no sound, not even from far away. Yet it seems that is what people are listening for—any sound coming from a distance. No one knows the source of the rumors that this is the day the planes will come. The rumors have been everywhere; yesterday evening, shortly after eight o'clock, there was a brief air-raid alert, telephones were ringing all over town, but nothing happened. Those were the planes Karadžić has asked for from Panić, with Milošević acting as an intermediary. There are reports confirming that Milošević intends to use his influence on the army's new commander in chief to make those planes appear in the skies above Sarajevo. After this became known, General Panić denied the rumor, claiming that it was "a blatant lie." Obviously this has agitated people even more. No one has forgotten how General Kukanjac, the commander of the armed forces stationed in Bosnia-Herzegovina at the beginning of the war, responded to reports on anything and everything that took place by stating that they were "the most blatant lies." In fairness, one must admit that there is one among those fellows who has never told a lie—the maniac Perišić, who kept his promise to the citizens of Mostar that he was going to destroy their town. Truly a man of his word.

In the midst of this calm, while the city is waiting for the planes or whatever else may come, I am told about something that happened yesterday. It says more about this city and its inhabitants than many more grandiose war stories. "Honored" by particularly heavy sniper fire, one residential section of Sarajevo experienced famine before it hit other parts of town. No one dared to stick his nose outside, much less venture out to the bread truck, for fear that the hyenas and their twins would indulge in a bloodbath.

Then someone had an idea. First, one person managed to get up on the roof of the building in which the sniper had installed himself, and lowered a plastic bag containing a loaf of black bread past the side of the sniper's window down to the next level, where another person attached a rock to the end of the line and managed to throw it to a neighbor waiting behind an open window in the building across the way. As soon as this line had been made taut between the two buildings, probably to the astonishment of the sniper who must have been watching, the bread bag was slid down along the line. Witnesses said that at one point it got stuck on the branch of a tree, but unexpectedly a long pole appeared out of a nearby window and sent the loaf on its way again. Finally understanding what was going on, the sniper opened fire, hoping to hit the bag or the line or whatever he could, but by then it was too late: the loaf had reached the window it was destined for. Deafening applause, shouts of joy, and a few shots that rang out from the surrounding buildings.

This is the story of Sarajevo and its proud citizens, who will bend neither their backs nor their heads. This is the story of their lives, resumed every morning in defiance of a subhuman horde. Of course not all Sarajevans are such heroes—among us there are many different kinds. But the streetcar conductors and bus drivers continue to do their job, traveling through the devastated city as long as their vehicles still run, without even asking for fares. There are bakers and dairymen stopped only by mortar shells. There are electricians, plumbers, and plain night owls who refuse to take notice of the war, as do many journalists, printers, and cameramen. But there are also those who've buried their heads in basements, even when there is no obvious danger; there are those who have departed without asking any questions. No, they are not to be reproached. Fear is, after all, a most human trait. But still, what matters most are the things that prevail, like this calm wait for the bombers, for example, and the invention of new tricks such as the loaf on a line. The life force, as soldiers would say, is a powerful thing, especially when it is in the right.

2 June 1992

TENNIS—LIFE AND DEATH

Among the news items received by the editorial desk of
Oslobodenje I find the following: "At a meeting held today in
Paris, the International Tennis Federation has decided to
postpone acceptance of a new rule that the game will
continue after a serve when a ball has touched the net and
fallen into the correct quarter of the court. According to
current rules, a ball that touches the net has to be followed
by a new serve. . . ."

At the same time, we receive appeals from Visoko,
Zenica, Tuzla, Breza, and the occupied quarters of Sarajevo, Dobrinja, and Butmir. They implore us to send news
summaries from the latest edition of our paper to a few
clandestine fax numbers, so that their inhabitants can learn
of yesterday's destruction—who has died, who has survived. Several readers from various parts of the world beg
us to let them know what is happening in Prijedor and in
Sanski Most, because they have heard that the *chetniks* have
perpetrated mass killings there, evicted the inhabitants
and burned their houses. Yesterday the news service *Srna*
did not add a single word of commentary to the news that
the felon Karadžić had announced to "his" people that
certain "Serb regions" could not be held as originally
envisaged, and that the indigenous population would have

to resign itself to a different solution from the one they had been counting on. At the same time, journalists at the International Press Center want to know, "When will Bosnia-Herzegovina's television start to use a terminology about this war that describes what is actually taking place?" (In the interest of moderation, Bosnian TV journalists have avoided naming the aggressor or any of the parties involved in the conflict.) Others believe that war terminology, or a warlike way of interpreting the news, adds nothing to the bald facts—the facts of war, the facts of peace. I agree, though I know that we are at war, and that all news is part of the context of this war.

But to return to the beginning. I wasn't particularly excited at our ability to receive, with such speed, the International Tennis Federation's opinions about balls that touch the net, and particularly what happens when a ball falls on the court inside the designated playing area. What moved me were the requests from many people all over Bosnia-Herzegovina who have a fax machine and who want to receive any information they can get from us, without doubting for a moment its veracity or reliability. I am moved to tears by the fact that day after day, in so many Bosnian towns, people form a line in front of the windows that display a single telefaxed copy of this newspaper. I am also excited by the fact that as of tomorrow, the metal workers of Zenica will start manufacturing a kind of pocket-size reprint of *Oslobodenje* to sell to their fellow citizens, who are eager to hear news from other parts of the republic.

The dispatch about the ball and the net, as well as the news of bloody events in Sarajevo, or Karadžić's statement that he has to renegotiate on promises made to his partisans (a statement they won't believe)—these all bear witness to the power, speed, significance, and importance of a medium of information that doesn't sugarcoat suffering and grief, doesn't leave room for regrets or moralizing, but simply relates events as they happen. The news, the facts, the truth work for us, independent of our personal passions, subjective opinions, and frustrations.

Today, after everything that has happened, a voice has reached us from Mostar, breaking the terrible silence from that ravaged town. Tomorrow, on a street corner of Mostar, in front of a picture window, someone will read about all of us and our battle.

That the rules of tennis refuse to change strikes us as quite ridiculous—considering the never-ending transformation of the rules of life and death in our country. Nonetheless, it is wonderful that we're able to receive such news quickly and efficiently from Paris. That means information sent out by us about what is happening here also stands a chance of getting through to the outside.

God bless information!

7 June 1992

CHILDREN AND
BLOCKS OF WOOD

The night before last someone said there were ten deaths in our building—of which not much more than a charred skeleton remains, and in which we produce our paper for the people in Sarajevo. The next morning the paper was once again for sale in the city streets. Today at dawn, after an hour's sleep on a stretcher, I was awakened by a phone call. Someone in the city was calling to ask:

"Will the paper be coming out today . . . ?"

"Of course it will—why shouldn't it? And it will come out tomorrow, and the day after, and every day after that. We'll print it in handwriting if we have to."

This morning, wide awake and angry, I came across an old copy of the paper and the following statement: "We must not leave it to a stranger to fire the bullets that kill *chetniks*. I do not want to share that pleasure with anyone. Imagine how sad it would be if a Belgian or a Kenyan killed Radovan Karadžić or Šešelj. . . ." These are the words of a member of an old Sarajevan family, a man who has built his whole life on the idea of tolerance, forgiveness, and a remarkably strong sense of attachment to his neighbors—

and who, what's more, has raised his children in the same spirit of tolerance.

There are many in Sarajevo whose thinking has changed in a similar way. They speak differently now, even though their actions, in spite of everything that has been done to them, still bear witness to their former generosity. Consider, for example, the case of the military musician who left the Marshal Tito Barracks with his outfit. The Sarajevans helped him when his car stalled in the middle of the departing column. They pushed the car, they tried to tow it, they tried to stop his comrades in arms marching past, but they kept going without paying any attention to what was happening behind them. Finally the Sarajevans attached the musician's car to a vehicle of the Bosnian police force, which then towed it until it caught up with the convoy that had abandoned him without even noticing.

They have destroyed our city, and no doubt they'll keep on ravaging what remains. But if I know my people, one day they'll be forgiven, though we will never forget what they have done. But what we'll neither forgive nor forget is that they have broken what was best in us; they have taught us to hate. They have made us become what we never were—and that is why, though they will be forgiven, we'll find it difficult to do so. It will be difficult for this ravaged Bosnia to return to what it used to be, with the people that we have become. And yet the way it used to be was the only way we knew. . . .

Never again will Bosnia be a paradise for those who straddled the fence, those who lowered their heads and lent their ears to the words of the great and powerful. We are not great and powerful. No longer will this be a hospitable terrain for clever bootlickers who knew how to shed their skin when it was convenient, while maintaining a facade of honesty.

A few days ago, late in the evening, one of my friends, a university professor and a cultivated man, heard an outcry from one of his friends in Belgrade—like him, a cultivated person and a humanist. Over the ham radio waves, the latter made the observation: "How could anyone possibly bomb Belgrade? Don't they know that we have children here?" My professor, a gentle dove in former days, replied coldly: "Here in Sarajevo, all we have is blocks of wood."

Nothing is the way it used to be, and it never will be again.

10 June 1992

THE LOGIC OF CHAOS

This morning, a little after five, a general alert was sounded. It is now almost nine, and the alert is still in effect. While the earth shakes, I note how irrational it is to speak of "general" danger. How ridiculous it is to wait for the "all clear," the end of danger, when days and nights in Sarajevo are all the same, when the city has been gutted. Here, danger has become permanent, and suffering inevitable. Nothing but uncertainty is certain. How could one define its beginning or end? There will be a definitive end to it all, and what that end will be is a matter of chance, in every case.

In these hours, days, and months, in which all of life depends on nothing but (mis)fortune, we find ourselves imperceptibly moving in new directions. At other times, in other places, these new directions might seem ridiculous.

New philosophies are born, designed for ourselves and our loved ones. Their objective is to guarantee survival, to protect oneself from oneself and one's fears. After a shell—one of dozens—exploded close by, I overheard a conversation between two of my huddled colleagues:

"I knew it was going to hit here. Igor is down there, he didn't want to stay."

"Come on, how did you know it was going to hit here? How was Igor supposed to know that?"

"Well, obviously he knew. People just know, everybody knows. . . ."

He's convinced himself: everybody knows. No one realizes that such "knowing" is pure nonsense. No one can ever know anything about this madness, because all its components are unknown. But we've been raised by our parents to look for a reason, always and everywhere, and for a black-and-white scheme of things. We've always known all the proper responses, and that made us feel strong, almost invincible. This makes the chaos that has overwhelmed us all the more painful, and for some of us, it proves fatal. No one knows how to respond to the real questions of today.

No one knows what is happening, or why, or who has a chance to survive and who doesn't. Where will the shell drop? Where are the safe places? Who will get in the way of a bullet? Who was born under a lucky star?

It is not surprising that everyone, without exception, searches for a logic, a meaning, a rule in the chaos that has become absolute and, it seems, infinite. Those who think they have found such a rule believe they "know" a lot of things: where to cross and at what moment, what roads are out of the question, what one can do without taking a risk, why the shells are falling here and not over there. These people are perfectly familiar with the rules of life that say who is more likely to win the lottery than be hit by a sniper's bullet. But the bullets whistle through Sarajevo every day, and only the newspapers tell us about the lottery winners, and their names aren't ours.

It's been a relentless morning. Shells are falling close by us, perhaps closer than ever before. The official alert remains in force; so does our private and personal alert. We evaluate our chances, run risks, and keep hoping. We need to find our strength in private ways—by learning not to lie to ourselves anymore, and not to look for logic where none exists. Because if we should find one, it would lead us to find a justification and a logic behind the actions of those who have destroyed all logic.

But I have to move now, because the noise has become unbearable. Once I've gone, you can be sure, I'll feel absolutely certain that a shell will soon hit the spot I've just left. But it won't hit where I'm going. I wouldn't be a true Sarajevan, full of sangfroid and flaming optimism, if I didn't believe that. Just as I know that soon this madness will all be over.

ON NEW HORIZONS

Yesterday afternoon, after staying at the office around the clock for eight days straight, our small band of journalists packed it in and went home. No one knows for how long. If the times weren't what they are, we would be heading for a two-week vacation, at the end of which we'd return to the same place, to perform the same tasks. But in these hectic times fourteen days has become a lifetime.

Today, eight days after we entered our towering building, which keeps getting smaller—and which we love the more for being bloody but unvanquished—the city no longer resembles the one we left. Some streets have simply disappeared; some street corners where we used to meet are no longer there; even some huge trees which for decades—no, centuries—blocked our view of the slopes of Trebević, are gone.

It has taken me all morning to understand why I can suddenly see from my window certain parts of the city I've never been able to see before. The answer is simple and stunning: buildings, walls, branches that always were part of my surrounding landscape have simply vanished. Thus, my universe expands from hour to hour.

For sixty uninterrupted hours they've been showering steel on our dear city, on our gardens and tree-lined streets, our courtyards and facades. In this inferno there is no truce, no rest, no abatement of the red-hot artillery pieces, not even any need to give orders or to say, "Yes, I get it; I understand." Death has installed himself on an assembly line and mocks us all without distinction.

Its best children are leaving, ever more rapidly and inexorably; they are leaving the Sarajevo for which we have felt such a particular and disinterested affection. Death picks them off one by one. What a monstrous lie it is to claim that *fortune favors the bold*. In Sarajevo it favors only cretins and madmen. Fortune is on the side of fools and savages. It can be bought or extorted only from those who have money and arms. We, who are so far from the heart of the world, don't have the money to buy it, nor are we willing to beg for it. That is why our horizons keep expanding hourly. Soon, very soon, nothing will obstruct the view, or the thoughts and feelings—in those who survive.

Sarajevo has been without electricity for days. The meager contents of our refrigerators have spoiled. For days there has been no running water, so the last bag of flour isn't much use. The telephone no longer works, and even if it did, whom would you call? It rained yesterday, but many of us didn't think to collect the water in pots and buckets. How would we think of collecting rainwater, after so many years in which water ran from the tap? But the next time it rains, if it does, we'll know what to do. As always, we'll know many things next time, if there is a next time.

While waiting, we save our last transistor batteries, we no longer listen to the world's perverse lies. Out there the boards of corporations and the directorates of cricket clubs are still ready to embark on the project of proposing a suggestion for a basis for an accord that will eventually permit them to name "all the parties to the conflict" in Sarajevo. Instead, we listen to the music of our friends who compose for us, for the city, and for themselves. And we sing together. The world will probably find it hard to understand our songs, because they're a little different from what is sung elsewhere. But it is also a good thing that we can't be understood; otherwise it might seem that something was amiss here—that, God forbid, we actually resembled the world that they know. That would be a true defeat—a total defeat. Here we have been left to our own devices, to our own songs. If we happen to meet someone in passing, we will wish them good day, with the knowledge that we're addressing a human being. But we will continue on our own way, making the best of what we've got.

13 June 1992

SPRING IN SARAJEVO

Believe it or not, I took a walk through town this afternoon. What's more, I walked to hills I'd never been to before. And I saw spring—greening courtyards, rosebushes, even cherry trees. In a garden, in the green shade of a tree, some people had taken out *fildjans** for Turkish coffee. They were just as surprised to spot a stranger on a stroll as I was to see them. But both they and I were equally sure it was unlikely one of "us" would run into "them" in such an idyllic spot, especially during a truce.

They invited me to drink coffee with them, pleased at the chance to talk to a journalist and ask questions. For my part, I was pleased not to have missed spring altogether, and to be reminded of the same time last year, when my wife Biljana, our sons, Dado and Ogi, and I walked around on the outskirts one Friday before a trip to Mostar, Ston, and Mala Luka, and on to the Pelješac peninsula on the Adriatic shore.

This year I came close to missing the foliage, the cherries, and the roses, having lived and worked in bunkers, in ravaged streets and torn-up parks, in strange neighborhoods—in a city slowly dying from its unwillingness to beg for alms.

*Small cups for drinking Turkish coffee.

Over the coffee, the best I've ever tasted, I was asked, "Mr. Journalist, tell us straight—is there going to be an end to all this? " They obviously thought I knew a little more about our troubles than they did. That I had more access to the inside story. They weren't aware that they knew better than anyone what *really* mattered, and that it is never a good idea to ask anything of a journalist. . . .

What they really wanted to know was what the foreigners were doing about this war—the Americans and the rest of the rich and powerful. The answer was, of course, nothing. Nothing today, nothing tomorrow. But how to tell that to these people drinking coffee in the sunshine, eating cake made without milk, eggs, or baking powder?

So I told them about Boutros Ghali, a man I had known and admired at another time and in another city, in Cairo. I respected him, and was delighted with his tender concern for his grandson, who was a classmate of my Ogi. I had thought of his move to New York, to the United Nations, as a victory of justice over evil. But then I had to tell my hosts that despite his best intentions and qualities, this excellent man was unable to do anything for us, even if he wanted to, because the story of Bosnia is small compared to the world's big stories, and, well, we were just a little too far away.

"It's true, his life can't be easy over there, among those wolves in America," said an old man. Until that moment he had sat there in silence, smoking some old tea rolled in paper. "If it were just up to him, he might help us. But let me tell you something. I have more confidence in my boys, Dino and Selim, than in this Ghali. Today they left for Vrace. There's no point in asking for favors. That just isn't our style. But tell us what you know about how our people are doing. And thanks for telling us about Ghali. How could he know what is going on here, when it's so far away."

Luckily I had something I was able to tell them. I knew that the night before a convoy carrying some heavy artillery to our fighters had crossed one of the surrounding hills. I also knew that today or tomorrow some of the sniper-infested buildings in Nedžarići, Lukavica, and Vrace would go up in flames. I said things would get even hotter in days to come, but that it had to be that way so things would get better later on. I had to tell them that "Operation Airport," at least the way it was conceived, was idiocy, a concession to the *chetniks*, since it allowed them to gain time (whether the Blue Helmets were aware of this or not). Time was of the essence for the *chetniks*; at this very moment they were busy destroying two or three districts of Sarajevo and several cities in Bosnia-Herzegovina.

As I left, my hostess slipped a small parcel of cakes in my hand: "Now remember to bring your family to see us, as soon as this is over. My Dino and my Selim say it won't last much longer." And my host added, "I feel bad for this Ghali, since he's such a fine person, as you say, Mr. Reporter. Maybe the man will be able to pull through this whole mess someday. Tell him, whenever you happen to see him again, that if he ever needs any help, we're ready. You know what we're like."

Now, back in the urban cauldron where things are going from bad to worse, I am haunted by a thought: It would have been a real pity to have missed spring, and these people of the Sarajevo spring. If I ever see my friend from Cairo again, we'll have something to talk about. And if I don't see him in my lifetime, I'm sure my son Ogi will talk to Ghali's grandson, his classmate. Old classmates have a way of running into each other.

17 June 1992

MOJMILO, THE HILL OF ACCUSATION

If one had any reserves left of malice and ill will, today would be the day to exhibit them, for the umpteenth time, to the rest of the world. The cease-fire, "Operation Airport," the retreat of the army, the humanitarian aid, and so on would provide excellent subjects for scorn and ridicule, because the mortar shells keep raining down just as they did when the world recognized, that there was fighting going on. On the runways of the airport, where the international experts arrived to "express their satisfaction with its condition before its reopening," tanks and armored cars are driving back and forth, mowing down everything within range of their murderous guns.

Several aid convoys had been thunderously announced, but what arrived were only two trucks, and even these had been plundered by "one of the parties of the conflict"—to use the cynical expression favored by those who profit from our suffering. Farther away, far from Sarajevo, "the army that has withdrawn from Bosnia-Herzegovina," aided by "the planes that no longer violate the air space of Bosnia-Herzegovina," is wiping out everything in its path. Drunken bearded criminals from Serbia and Montenegro arrive to take the place of the dead, the disappeared, and the deserters.

Nevertheless, the situation has changed a little, at least as far as Sarajevo is concerned. Since yesterday, the city has acquired a witness. A small, taciturn, battered, but still unconquered witness—the hill of Mojmilo that rises between the suburb of Dobrinja, the airport, and the Lukavica barracks. From there one has a view of the runways of the airport, of the Nedžarići barracks, the *Oslobodenje* building, and even more distant landmarks. What's more, it is a place from which one can view the crimes that have been committed. Hence it wasn't surprising that the humanoids guarded and defended it as energetically and as long as they did. But from the moment they had to abandon it, Mojmilo became a leading witness for all the trials to come—trials of the criminals who have destroyed, burned, razed, and annihilated, but also of those who have proved to be indifferent, uncommitted, impartial, and handcuffed by their principles: the fans of "international procedure," who, when they came to visit Sarajevo, allowed themselves to be put up by the wild animals in the Lukavica barracks, instead of coming to stay with the real people in the city.

As long as Mojmilo was still in the hands of the federals, the last soldiers to defend it under that flag were young and inexperienced, but loyal to the population living at the foot of the hill. A month ago they let several thousand refugees from Dobrinja "pass," and the *chetniks* couldn't forgive them for that. They killed all of those young boys and occupied the hill so they could fire on anyone who came within range down below.

In the end, at last, the Bosnian flag with its golden fleurs-de-lis was raised on Mojmilo, and from there images were transmitted to the entire world: the gaping holes in the buildings of the Olympic village; the dead bodies in the streets that no one had dared to retrieve; the graves dug out in front of apartment buildings; the tanks driving up and down the runways and firing at whatever they please; the furiously revolving turrets of armored vehicles, spewing record-breaking numbers of rounds into the air; the houses of criminals like Tintor, Trapar, Sucur, and others, which Sarajevo will raze in retribution for what they have done to it.

Liberated today, Mojmilo can also testify to the columns of innocents who have been transported in trucks for days to the Lukavica barracks and the old Kula ("Tower") restaurant, buildings that have been transformed into concentration camps. These people are considered guilty because they aren't Serbs, or because they don't want to be Serbs of the kind that pleases Milošević. What will those who defend the thesis of "shared responsibility" say, now that the camera mounted on Mojmilo shows them the tanks and armored vehicles? When they see how a Slovenian journalist and an American journalist were wounded by their fire; when they realize that the young Slovenian could have been saved? The camera at Mojmilo shows very clearly the connection between that event and the barricade erected by the bearded criminals. It shows all those things—unless it too is a liar, like everybody else. . . .

No, gentlemen, leaders of a shameless world, there can be no more lying here. Take your money and get out, if you can't act with integrity. We may, of course, disagree on the definition of the word "integrity." But now the hills are on our side. Climb Mojmilo and take a look. Right now, or a little later. It would be better if you did it sooner rather than later—better for us, and, it seems to me, better for you too.

18 June 1992

THE "UN-PROTECTION FORCE"

We've gotten used to life's disappointments, we've even gotten the hang of it. Maybe our problem is that we used to expect too much. I mean of life. So that now, when life itself is worthless, the possibility of being let down is even greater. But you must make do with what you have; there are more important things to worry about than simple expectations. We'll get to them later, if there is a later.

Nevertheless, it is hard to ignore that another illusionary bubble has burst here in Sarajevo and maybe even farther, beyond Sarajevo. This illusion we called the UNPROFOR, or, loosely translated, the United Nations protection and peace-keeping force in the former Yugoslavia.

In a few months, the Blue Helmets, once the darlings of Sarajevo, have become targets of resentment and scorn. They have also come to symbolize international hypocrisy and political dirty dealing. In the beginning, people would approach these boys in the street and shake their hands. They were welcomed with applause in the cafés, people treated them with sympathy, even love. Now those feelings have turned, in some cases one hundred eighty degrees:

"Maybe if General MacKenzie were assassinated, they'd finally understand what is going on here. . . ." Obviously, the *chetniks* have no reason to set their sights on *him*.

It is also obvious that the UN forces obey their own rules, and that these are more rigid than our own notions of order, neutrality, and professionalism. But we've become used to that. And it goes without saying that you can't expect them to put their heads on the line while we're busy settling our internal accounts and other varied stupidities. Still, one has the right to expect from them a sense of justice that corresponds with the basic principles of the organization they represent and are financed by. Sadly, such an expectation is not borne out by the facts.

General MacKenzie and his immediate superior Marrack Goulding, also known here as "Slobodan Milošević's last official comrade," declared today that "conditions have not been met for the realization of the second phase of Operation Airport." In other words, the *chetniks* are still bombarding the city from emplacements on the airport runway. They are still deporting thousands of people from Grbavica, Dobrinja, and the airport suburb, taking them to camps established all around the outskirts of Sarajevo, while tanks descend the slopes of Trebević and move closer to the center of town.

Yesterday, before the cameras, General MacKenzie coolly declared that he was not interested in knowing *who* had broken the cease-fire agreement. He said that all he knew was that the airport could not be reopened as long as the fighting continued. It's been a long time since such blatant hypocrisy has been seen around here in public. The General waits for terrorists to decide, of their own free will, to stop being terrorists, so that peace operations may begin—to the detriment of their ambitions, but with their blessing!

For those who still find themselves unable to make sense of MacKenzie's statements (which are apparently dictated to him by the UN's New York headquarters), here is a bit of news, as outlandish as it might seem: While the *chetnik* tanks (property of the "Yugoslav" army) stationed at the airport are sowing death in the homes of Sarajevo, a few UN vehicles are also stationed in front of the airport, and a few Blue Helmets have been spotted playing soccer in the vicinity of their vehicles.

While credence can't be given to all the rumors you hear about this "mythical" army of the UN, indisputable facts can't go ignored. The white protection force vehicles have consistently refused to help women and children leave besieged Dobrinja, even when they had reached the end of their rope. "It's against the rules."

Nevertheless, the same vehicles have conveyed Mrs. Biljana Plavsic and her family out of the city. This, it seems, did not conflict with their rules. On several occasions, these vehicles and those in charge of them have been "arrested" and "detained" in the *chetnik* strongholds at Pale and Lukavica. It turns out, however, that the Blue Helmets had chosen to go there to spend the night, where they were the beneficiaries of "protection" and who knows what else.

Is it necessary to point out, once again, that Lukavica, the site of their visit, is also the site of imprisonment for more than a thousand innocent civilians who have been brought there from the "conquered territories" to serve as a human shield against attacks on that stronghold?

Is international public opinion aware of the price of a ride out of town in one of the UNPROFOR's vehicles?

Sarajevans certainly are. It is one hundred German marks, cash, counted out into a Blue Helmet's palm. Dozens of witnesses can confirm this, particularly along the road leading to Fojnica, for example.

But that's the way it is with illusions. The only question is what you do when they're shattered. We are insignificant pawns in the great game played by Europe and the United States, by Ghali, Goulding, and who knows who else.

All we can do at this time is to watch and remember. We tell them what we call them here: Smurfs, or simply the Un-Protection Force.

19 June 1992

NO FORGIVENESS FOR
HUMILIATION

It has been a long time since Sarajevo has wept over its fate or wailed about the shells raining down upon it. In Sarajevo, frustration has replaced tears. There are times when black humor seems the most appropriate response to the misery inflicted upon us by the mortar and artillery shells. The anxiety this shelling causes takes precedence over every other concern. We're all preoccupied with learning how to recognize, automatically, the caliber of death, by gauging the length of the whistle, its type, and the point of origin of the explosion. Everybody seems to have become an expert at evaluating degrees of danger. Sometimes it is enough to seek shelter behind a provisional barrier, sometimes one may have to stay put for several minutes. There are times when you have to stick your head as deep into the ground as possible. Miscalculations of this kind are, naturally, hard to rectify.

Sad as it may seem, the city as a whole reacts less and less emotionally to the destinies of those who haven't had the skill, or the luck, to gauge the trajectory of a shell or the position of a sniper correctly. Grief has become a private matter. It's as if the tears of collective grief have dried up, or they've been put aside for some other time. If that time comes.

The only place that all Sarajevo's eyes have focused on is that abominable collective nightmare called Lukavica. Until yesterday it was only a barracks on the outskirts of town. Since yesterday it is a stain on the conscience of the world, especially on the conscience of what calls itself twentieth-century Europe—a concentration camp in the most literal sense of the word. One of the "parties to the conflict" (as the commanders and officials of the United Nations put it, with such loathsome hypocrisy) has arrested, loaded onto trucks, and deported to Lukavica more than two thousand people. These people have nothing to do with the conflict; it is merely their misfortune to have been born of a Muslim, Croat, or "wayward" Serb mother. Brutally, savagely, just the way we used to see in movies about the Gestapo and the Jews, they've been chased out of their apartments and herded into those trucks by men making good use of their rifle butts. For two months they had been practically imprisoned in their apartments (because they lived in "foreign territory," within their own city). Now they have been taken to the barracks, or, more precisely, the stables of those barracks, which are the headquarters of the monstrous Mladić and Karadžić the psychopath. At the same time, with increasing frequency, the barracks are also serving as the *home sweet home* of UN dignitaries. To this day, as they continue to transport truckloads of people to a concentration camp next to the airport, seventy-five days after the beginning of the bombardment of Sarajevo, the UN is still trying to figure out who is doing the shooting.

In this city where people meet violent deaths every day, and life no longer seems the highest good, death has become something to be expected, something logical, if you will. There is a tacit understanding that all it takes is a little bad luck. In order to fit all this dying into a context of manifest madness, you must relativize the notion of death. Proceeding from this view, you may reach a point of forgiveness beyond thoughts of vengeance.

But to forgive the humiliation of deportations to a concentration camp—that is not possible in Sarajevo, nor will it ever be. When a bullet in the back ends your life, there's nothing left—no distress, nor any consciousness of distress. The rifle butt in the back, and the truck ride to the camp, cause a distress that cannot be forgotten. That rifle butt shatters everything civilization has ever accomplished, removes all finer human sentiments, and wipes out any sense of justice, compassion, and forgiveness.

Killings might be considered acceptable in times of war, but deportations go beyond warfare. Deportation is the ultimate humiliation that can be inflicted on a human being. No one can go on living with the memory of it without a desire for revenge.

Whatever the ultimate fate of the several thousand uprooted Sarajevans turns out to be, their deportation has extinguished all gentle and humanitarian feelings in tens of thousands of their fellow citizens. Evil has multiplied in the worst way. Sarajevo is no longer a city that suffers; it has become a city that is waiting for revenge. In these parts, death has always been pardonable, but humiliation—never. When all this passes, may their mothers lament for them, if they were actually borne by mothers.

20 June 1992

A NICE SUNNY DAY

Here it is, Saturday, the first day of summer. A moment ago the announcer on duty at Sarajevo's Center for Security had this to say: "The city is relatively calm. A few shells have hit the district of Marindvor, and two or three buildings have been destroyed. From the Lukavica barracks missiles have been fired at the *Oslobodenje* building, and anyone who has no urgent reason for being in that area is advised to stay away for at least an hour. We will let you know when the area is safe again. You are advised to avoid long lines in front of bakeries or district offices that distribute ration cards; the rocket launchers are aimed at targets where people congregate. Electricity and water services are still interrupted, but we are working on their restoration. Don't leave your homes unless it is absolutely necessary. You have heard the sirens sound a general alert. Otherwise, it is a nice sunny day. . . ."

What can one tell the world about Sarajevo on this nice sunny day? Nothing. Those who want to know about Sarajevo already know. Those who wish to ignore what is happening here will continue turning a deaf ear. It would be pointless to bother them. We'll keep ourselves from getting too excited anymore, because agitation reduces your ability to deal with life's small but fundamental challenges. Such as, for instance, how to get a light source, or, for that matter, electricity. The last few days Sarajevans have been searching in hundreds of wrecked, smashed, or completely destroyed cars for batteries that still hold a charge. If a headlight has survived, it can be connected to the battery and used to light a room. It goes without saying that this is of interest only to those fortunate enough to have a room that is still habitable.

Yesterday evening I returned to my apartment in the company of a couple of friends. I didn't dare tell them where I had found a battery, but it was in good shape, and large. I also had had the windfall of finding a brand-new bicycle lamp that was originally intended for my son's bike. True, it was a little difficult to make it work (it was built in China and bought in Egypt . . . there's a mix of Oriental technology for you!), but finally we managed to. My "lodger," Goran, an electronics engineer and a refugee from Dobrinja, refreshed his memory of basic electrician-ship, and compared to most everyone else we are now masters of the art. The hardest part of our enterprise was to smuggle the battery in without anyone noticing. We wanted to avoid an earlier mistake of Goran's; he had brought home, in a transparent plastic bag, four eggs that he had gotten in exchange for a couple of cigarettes. For the next two days neighbors kept coming by asking us where we had gotten those eggs. God alone knows what would have happened if they'd known that we had cigarettes. . . .

Since it is the first day of summer, and as the announcer of the Center for Security has informed us, a nice sunny one, we are going to celebrate by trying to bake some bread in a pressure cooker. Some friends to whom we revealed our secret source of electricity and light told us what to do. We have the basic requirement—we can still find a little bit of gas. They say that you can purchase those little canisters for two kilos of Vegeta*. The only thing is, where will I be able to find Vegeta? But after we're done with all these, shall we say, domestic chores, we hit the streets again, everyone going only as far as he deems prudent, and in a calm and noncompetitive way. Some make it as far as the carriage entrance, some all the way to the next district. It pays to move around, otherwise you can't get anything accomplished.

Yesterday we heard that someone nearby was selling batteries for transistor radios at the bargain price of two thousand dinars apiece. Four batteries of different sizes, wrapped in a rubber band, represent a month of radio news. We no longer listen to music or commentaries or reviews of the foreign press. We know all that. The only thing we listen to is the news, particularly from the Center of Security. If we hadn't listened to it today, we wouldn't have known that it was such a nice sunny day. . . .

We didn't have to listen to the news to know that summer has begun; we can hear the detonations. We can feel the walls tremble. God, what is happening to our loved ones?

*A popular spice mix used to flavor cooked foods.

21 June 1992

OSLOBODENJE IN FLAMES

Now they imagine they've achieved their objective at last. Yesterday the sky was in flames above Nedžarići, the district many Sarajevans know mainly by the landmark building of *Oslobodenje*. The red sky above Nedžarići marked the demise of that great edifice, and it must have pleased the pyromaniacs of "one of the parties to the conflict" to no end. At the same time, however, it also confirmed a truth we have repeated many times over the last few weeks: *Oslobodenje* has emerged victorious, as it was bound to, because its existence does not depend on the building that burned, nor does it depend on the spared location, the place from which, this morning, a new issue appeared, its price doubled from yesterday's.

The Sarajevans, many of whom are too poor to afford bread (when bread is available), bought up the entire edition in one hour. The typical reaction we heard to what had happened to us, including from some who spent the night trying to put out the fire, was, "God, it's great to know they hate you so much that they're willing to use up all that ammunition, over so many days, just to hurt you. Imagine what you must have done to them, for them to consider you so important. . . ."

In other times we might have reacted differently to the

fire that devoured our home. We would have grieved over the superb work spaces we had dreamt about for forty years and enjoyed for a decade. We would have talked about all the computers, all the machines and printing equipment that had remained in there and would never again be used to set a word; or we would have lamented the loss of Zuka Džumhur's manuscripts, Adi Mulabegović's caricatures, Mario Mikulić's and Mica Todorović's photographs, all destroyed in the conflagration lit by imbeciles and aided by machine-gun fire whose sole purpose was to prevent us from putting it out.

But these aren't other times, these are the times we live in now. We won't weep for the building. Others more beautiful and more important already have gone up in flames. The Sarajevans are shedding tears because of what happened yesterday: The inhabitants of Dobrinja were subjected to merciless machine-gun fire by whoever had stolen some white armored vehicles belonging to the United Nations Protection Force. Those makeup artists in blue helmets didn't even bother to inform us who had stolen these vehicles, didn't even let us know that they had been stolen. Tears of rage were shed at certain words uttered by General MacKenzie, who said, imagine this, that the UN force will stop its efforts to reopen the airport unless "the two parties do not agree to a cease-fire of forty-eight hours." Further cause for tears are the dead bodies of persons killed this morning by mortar shells, in places where people have already died. Who hasn't heard about the shell that landed today on Vasa Miskin street, just like some time ago, in the middle of a breadline, hitting two mothers? What does the *Oslobodenje* building matter to children whose mothers will never return? Besides, we don't need that building now. We have our paper, and we have Sarajevo, a city that needs our paper. We are still here, safe and sound.

In the days to come, *Oslobodenje* may appear in a smaller format, and it may not have as many pages; we haven't made any final decisions about that. But there are some things that need no discussion: This paper, even if it's smaller and thinner, will go on printing everything that excites the hatred of idiots, but there will no longer be anything they could destroy. Imagine our joy! Our paper will report everything that causes that hypocrite Mac-Kenzie as well as Ghali and Goulding to go on fantasizing on the subject of "parties in conflict." One day, they'll be ashamed of those fantasies. As for us, we'll go on producing and preserving our paper. We'll hold on to our paper, and we'll even know how to produce reprints, to refresh the memories of those whose memories will need to be refreshed.

25 June 1992

THE LONG GOODBYE

That's what this war is, nothing but a long goodbye. You say goodbye to your illusions and your past, your dreams, your habits, hopes, and projects, all things great and small, and all the places inseparable from days gone by. You even say goodbye to the simple things that make up a life. But above all, you take your leave from many, many people, who are divided into two entirely separate camps, connected only by the thread that will join them forever: the war.

The first is made up of people who are no longer with us because death has chosen them. The second consists of those who have decided, out of stupidity or cruelty, or perhaps just out of weakness or laziness, to side with the eternal misfits and outcasts from the community of honest, just, and courageous men and women.

Yesterday marked a formal, definitive separation from several of the latter, old friends and colleagues among them. To say "formal and definite" may seem incongruous at a time when even the line that separates life from death has become blurred. But never again will we work together on the same newspaper, never again will we meet in the same Sarajevo cafés—at least not around the same table. And finally, never will we honor the solemn oath we swore only two months ago, to reunite in ten years, regardless of everything, and see how everyone has grown and changed.

Some of those who appear in our ten-year-old photographs have forced us to say goodbye, because it has become impossible for us to keep company with them. Not only for reasons of our own, but because of all the Sarajevans who have stepped on mines and come to a bloody end, and because of our children, who one day will ask us who our real friends are, and where they were when times were hard.

It would be dishonest of me to pretend that my heart doesn't ache because of this. We belong to the same generation. For years we spent our evenings together, and sometimes even woke up together. We worshiped the same deities and rejected the same saints, forgave one another when we could, and forgot what was unforgivable. We shared our lives all those years, and yet here we stand divided. On one side are those who have won their battle with the past and with the malevolent fate that has governed these lands; on the other, those who have been vanquished by their own shadows and by the evil they weren't able to resist. We can no longer walk the same road because they were not able to make peace with themselves—that is their tragedy.

The letters of dismissal addressed to the lost sheep of *Oslobodenje* may be the ultimate proof that we have been nurturing an illusion for most of our lives. On the positive side, it must be said that the line of separation did not fall along lines of mere herd allegiance; along these lines my old friends are divided among themselves. Our separation was caused by humanitarian values of the kind that are of no concern to people who have never left their cages.

Nevertheless, I regret the choice my old friends have made, as I regret my disillusionment over our friendship. I am afflicted by a terrible feeling of betrayal, and this in itself may be sufficient punishment for my illusions. As for them, they'll have to pay a far heavier price. They, whose sons and daughters are now in their early teens, are confronted by two alternatives: to teach these children to hate us and all normal people, in order to conceal the inhumanity that has cut them off from the rest of the world, or one day to have their children ask them questions that they would prefer left unasked.

What they've done to themselves, to their children, and to us is terrible. As for us, we're the least of the problem. I forgive them everything. I'm sorry for them. Life will take care of the rest.

26 June 1992

A WORD OF HONOR

Have you heard the blackest bit of humor making the rounds since yesterday? Radovan Karadžić has promised General MacKenzie that his artillery will no longer be directed against civilian targets. However, he has also informed the General that the city center of Sarajevo is "a military target, since arms are stored at the Presidential building of Bosnia-Herzegovina." So Karadžić's promise doesn't apply to that part of town. To compound the absurdity, the slap-happy general made a television appearance to announce what he presumably regards as a diplomatic victory, and the announcement has been carried by numerous international news networks.

Unfortunately, my friend Rešo Torlak was not aware of this new *pax Karadžićiana*. For many years a number of mutual friends, who are now leading the good life in Belgrade, were frequent patrons of his restaurant. Yesterday, Reso and his seven-year-old son Neno went out to buy some bread, some of the blood-stained bread of Sarajevo. One of the mortar shells that, according to Karadžić's word of honor, are no longer aimed at civilian targets, found one. Reso, a huge fellow, did his best to cover little Neno with his own body, but a small area of the child's head remained unprotected. Yesterday Sarajevo observed the boy's funeral, and my friend's life is hanging by a thread. I ask myself if this news, which must have reached Belgrade by now, cast a pall on some festive moment among those who were wined and dined innumerable times, on the house, at Reso's—like, for instance, on the day of Neno's birth.

General MacKenzie, after giving us his word of honor that there will be a cease-fire, also had this to say: "If the Serbs do not keep their promise this time, we'll consider it a serious violation of our trust on their side." Congratulations, General, for your stoic trust in "one of the sides of the conflict." And in order to preserve that trust, you will now have to announce that the armored vehicles that yesterday opened fire once again on Dobrinja and the area of the airport were of Bosnian provenance. Who else has armored vehicles here except the Green Berets, Alija's Soldiers? Furthermore, when your soldiers retreat again toward Belgrade, they will once again discover hundreds of deported Serbs imprisoned in the Lukavica barracks where they are being mistreated by Muslims and Croats. It will also be clear to you that little Neno, just like that other boy, Sdravko Hadžić, was killed by a "land mine" called "word of honor." You, General, must also know what your guru Slobodan Milošević told the charming Lord Peter yesterday: "Serbia and the Serbs are in no way involved in the war in Bosnia-Herzegovina." Later, over a whisky on the rocks, he may have added, "and even if they should be just a tiny bit involved, no one has any right to bother them. . . ."

So that's the way it is. On this "calm day" the shells are falling only on "military targets." Among those must be counted Sarajevo's largest residential suburb, Dobrinja, as well as the center of the city. These are the notorious "military targets," registered as such by all the military intelligence services of the world. Otherwise, everything is fine. There is absolutely nothing left to buy. Even the black market has closed down. This morning I encountered some characters offering fifteen hundred Yugoslav dinars for one German mark. I offered them stamps recovered from old letters, but they weren't interested (in Serbo-Croat, the word for "stamp" is *marka*). Their sense of humor left something to be desired. If that indicates a trend, things may get rough around here.

The presidency of Bosnia-Herzegovina has announced that one of its members, Ejup Ganić, is recovering from an appendectomy. We still don't know the state of recovery of all the casualties with amputated arms and legs, whose number has been established in only four districts of the city: seven hundred forty-four so far.

STRAW DOGS

It seems they can't take the rain. The whole night and all day today it's been raining cats and dogs, and, at least according to all the signs, they're not feeling too good over there in the hills, behind their guns. Since the rain started they háve been shelling the city only every fifteen minutes, for the hell of it, just so we don't forget they're around. Poor slobs; don't they know there's nothing they could do that would erase them from our memories?

One day, when all this is over, my friends Braco and Memica, now imprisoned (for the last two months) with their families in their homes in Dobrinja, will do something memorable. I don't know yet what it will be, and I doubt that they know. But whatever it is, I'm all for it.

The drama taking place in Dobrinja—which was once the site of the journalists' village during the Winter Olympics, those long-forgotten Winter Olympics—is unprecedented in recent times. Twenty thousand people, mainly chidren of the city who entered middle age and moved to the suburbs (near the airport, since the fat-assed wild people of the hills managed to buy their way into the center of town, pushing the old residents and their kids to the periphery), now find themselves in a real concentration camp, in the classic sense of the term. Karadžić, Mladić, and evidently even Milošević have made Dobrinja a "trump card in the negotiations." I'm sure that's how they think of it now, on the eve of the negotiations that Carrington, Cutilheiro, and the other international buffoons intend to pursue on the question of us. But they are thinking of times gone by, when Sarajevo was still a city.

In the meantime, day by day, the tale of Dobrinja becomes more epic, an argument against the blind who don't understand that a campaign to create impossible divisions cannot succeed. Encircling it with their steel, the savages have plunged Dobrinja into famine, disease, and total exhaustion.

For months the children of Dobrinja have had only sugarless tea to drink, if you can call a concoction of herbs and boiled leaves "tea." The inhabitants break up furniture and floorboards in order to heat their apartments, and then handfuls of flour are fried on that fire in whatever grease can be found. Re-boiled weeds or leftover tea bags, reused ten times over, are dried in the sun for "cigarettes." We who live in the center of town, in our basements and ruins, feel ashamed as we lament the loss of our meagre supplies, spoiled when we lost our electricity, once we remind ourselves of how people are living in Dobrinja.

And these idiots posted on the hills believe that my friends and all the other Dobrinjans will serve as a trump card in the negotiations. A trump card for whom, negotiations over what?

What they don't know is that since yesterday, people are singing again in that desperate, famished suburb. That they are producing handwritten leaflets, and somehow manage to duplicate them. That they even have a working fax on which, page by page, they get *Oslobođenje* and clippings from the foreign press. Then all this information moves under cover of darkness, from window to window, balcony to balcony. They don't know that the decision *We'll stay in Dobrinja until the end* is a solemn oath. You can't bargain with these people. They're not jokers, nor mice to be crushed, nor people without a vision of what Sarajevo is and what it will be.

The psychopath Karadžić thought that he could empty out Dobrinja, install his partisans there, and invite others to come who would be glad to take over the houses of the expelled. Everyone knows that there are many in Milošević's and Karadžić's camp who would be glad to settle themselves down in houses, apartments, and beds that don't belong to them.

But this won't work in Dobrinja. Do you remember the movie *Straw Dogs* and the character played by Dustin Hoffman, defending what was his by right? What do these savages think? That we'll just leave Sarajevo and go into refuge, into exile, into a home that isn't ours? Why, and to what end? Because a madman has conned the world into treating him like a politician, the leader of a party and a people? Such nonsense may trick an oversated world rumored to be suffering from senility. But it doesn't work here in Sarajevo, and among the "happy Bosnians," like most of the people in Sarajevo, it never will.

29 June 1992

THE SPARE WHEEL

We've finally gotten used to people dying for no good reason, and we no longer look for any logic in day-to-day events. Now we must accept that hope is equally pointless. The blue flag is flying above the airport, Blue Helmets are stationed around the runway. But only a couple of hundred yards away stand a great number of hostile black artillery pieces.

Tanks and artillery have been withdrawn from the airport? A fairy tale, or a bald-faced lie. Except, evidently, for those who trust reports issued by the United Nations more than they trust their own eyes. Yesterday evening and this morning we were able to see with our own eyes, here in Sarajevo, that the airport remains inaccessible. Their tanks are now installed in trenches next to the airport, and their guns are aimed at the airport and at the residential suburb of Dobrinja. The imperturbable Blues are watching, from a distance of twenty yards, an armored vehicle firing incessantly at Dobrinja. Today as yesterday, sticking one's neck out means risking one's life.

I don't know what the thousand Canadian soldiers who are coming to provide "logistical support" for "Operation Airport" will do when they get here. But I do know that no one here dares to ask when we'll have free access to the sea, when there will be free traffic between the different parts of the city where our relatives live, when it will be possible again to walk the streets after ten o'clock in the evening—even just for fun. If anyone believes that the opening of a runway that makes it possible to bring flour and rice into the city will take care of Bosnia's problems, they do not understand the situation.

It is a situation that must be remedied, and it doesn't matter how. That may sound brutal, but so is the reality we're living in. There are things we want at all cost—much more than we want flour. If we can no longer have them, because someone has already promised certain gentlemen "uncontaminated air" for the Serb sections in Pale, then they should let us know.

This morning, a street-cleaning operation was suddenly begun in the center of town. Employees of the parks department mowed the grass (where did they get the diesel fuel for their lawn mowers?), swept mounds of broken glass off the sidewalks, and collected kilometers of cable dangling down into the street, the remains of the electric network for streetcars and trolleys. Trucks carrying tons of garbage crisscrossed the city, and the dismal intersections of our streets began to look a little more presentable.

Someone must have felt bad about showing Mitterand a devastated city. What will he think of us! No, we can't let that happen with the British dignitary when *he* comes to pay us a visit. We're known the world over for our hospitality, aren't we? True, we're feeling a bit down in the mouth, but that doesn't mean we have to exhibit a dilapidated city to foreigners. If we do things right, maybe we'll be permitted to become members of a society where well-kept flower beds are considered more important than the psychological desert inside. That's called *civilization*, or so we hear.

It may be time to bid farewell to our old ways of life. Not long ago my friend Minja told me, not without a degree of wistfulness, "We just have to do what you do when a tire blows out. You put on the spare and drive on." The only problem is that this can't be done here in Bosnia. There are no more roads to drive on. There are no more spare tires.

Today began with a curiously normal feeling. The weather was nice. The shooting didn't exceed our habitual quota. We weren't lied to any more or less than usual. The obituaries read just the same. Then, all of a sudden, a man was killed under the windows of *Oslobodenje*. Who knows, maybe tonight someone will manage to go out and retrieve and identify him. Or if not tonight, someday soon. Provided that one of the white UNPROFOR vehicles that keep driving past doesn't completely crush him. Where are they going, anyway, all these UNPROFOR vehicles? They must be driving back and forth between the neatly mowed lawns at the center of town and the "open" airport, where soon, we are told, all that flour, and sugar, and perhaps even some Coca-Cola-flavored candy bars, will arrive.

1 July 1992

EYES AND EARS

General Louis MacKenzie, the justice-loving Canadian who is the commander of Sarajevo's "Operation Airport," announced last night that no planes will be allowed to land until further notice. He said that there was fighting at Dobrinja, and as long as the fighting continued, the General kept repeating, there would be no operation, no Blue Helmets, no benevolent foreign involvement on behalf of peace. This we were told in no uncertain terms.

Some clearheaded local journalists have revealed what is really going on. The *chetniks* have received permission to traverse the runway of the airport controlled by the General. They have installed their tanks in trenches beside stone walls running the length of the runway. And lies have been disseminated on the origin of shots fired at the poor Blues. All of this is news to the public abroad, and even here. No Canadian general can go on juggling the facts. It seems that the foreign media's "sacred respect for truth" is definitely over, as far as Sarajevo is concerned. Besieged, terrorized, isolated, and systematically decimated, Sarajevo has to see, hear, and think for itself. And Sarajevo has to see, hear, and differentiate clearly between those who have come to honor their obligation to truth and their profession, and those who came to make a pile of money out of our misery.

Yesterday a well-known reporter working for a large international news agency spent the night in our editorial office, where we insist on producing our newspaper, only a few hundred meters from the front and in a building that is close to collapsing. A colleague told me, "Don't mention her name—it's unprofessional to wash someone's dirty laundry in public."

This journalist had found herself close to the front with no way to get back to the center of the city. We offered her everything we had. All our latest information, a bit of our food, a reddish, sparse, salty, warm stew—though, I'm afraid, no meat, salad, or wine. Later we also gave her one of our army cots. We don't really sleep, anyway. She also had the use of our last flashlight to make her way through our long, dark hallways, where you have to wade knee-deep in broken glass.

Until late at night she listened to our collaborators who were calling us with their ham radios or over the few remaining telephone lines. She didn't say much and looked a little suspicious. We didn't try to convince her of anything. What would we have gained by making her believe us rather than MacKenzie? She wouldn't have been the first or last person who spent a night here and left still a skeptic.

In the morning she accepted the single cup of coffee we could offer; she watched our reporters arrive from the city, dodging sniper bullets. Those bullets had killed a colleague practically on our doorstep the day before. She saw them pick up stacks of newspapers and hurry out into the city to sell them. She heard the news that a colleague's car had rolled over in an intersection, struck by machine gun fire; she saw everything we did to get him out of the car, to take him to the hospital, and finally, happily, to his home. She saw two other colleagues hurry to salvage the newspapers that had been in that vehicle—after the driver, the papers were the most important thing. We could always find more cars. . . .

Finally, she heard me talk to a "connection" I have in France who wants to send us some aid. She heard me tell him that we didn't need bullet-proof vests or military equipment, we didn't need food, we didn't need anything but the twenty-two tons of newsprint he told me could be loaded onto a truck. Not a gram of anything else, except for a box of batteries, so that we could hear others and they could hear us.

After all that, the well-known reporter of a major international agency packed her bag, because a member of the special units of the Bosnian Territorial Defense Force had arrived to give her safe escort into the city. Before she left, she told me, "After this experience I can only go home and look for another kind of work. They've destroyed everything for me." "What did they destroy? And who do you mean?" "The men in uniform at Lukavica, and those of the UNPROFOR. I realize now that everything I've been writing has been completely wrong. God, what lies they have told me!"

Then she left. We didn't put any ideas into her head. All we did was give straight answers to questions that, every now and then, she asked us.

As for General MacKenzie, this morning he issued another statement. What he was talking about, we have no idea. About the airport, we use our own eyes and ears. It is a good thing to have eyes and ears, and to be able to trust them. My only regret is that we weren't able to offer the well-known reporter anything better for supper. Even our supplies of bicarbonate of soda are running low.

CANNED GOODS

There are Sarajevans who already know which canned meats are better, the ones from Italy or Germany. They know the difference between packaged butter and plain margarine. But many others, the vast majority, still haven't seen any canned meat, nor have they tasted the foreign butter. What's more, the latter can't understand how the former know these things. I feel sorry for them.

Neither my friends nor myself have seen any canned goods yet, but we know where the profiteers get them. They get them from the same place they get gas to drive around the ravaged city. It's where you can also have your telephone line repaired, when this is impossible anywhere else. It's where you can find meat when most people have forgotten what meat looks like.

That's life. That's war. That's reality for the people here, and it's the same the world over. The illusion of collective heroism, collective honesty, anything collective at all has not survived. In Sarajevo it has collapsed like a house of cards, even though this time of war is a time of collective suffering, and feelings are shared in a way that wouldn't be possible in normal times.

Today, as yesterday, Sarajevo is a city of people like any other, heroes and weaklings, cowards and scoundrels great and small, pickpockets and big-time criminals. Some have taken to wartime conditions like ducks to water, others are crushed by their worries to the point of paralysis and despair.

Such a city, like every other city in the world, has its own mind, its own logic, and it won't stand to have its common sense ravaged the way some, apparently, think. Honest or dishonest, no Sarajevan takes these flagrantly manipulative gifts of canned goods at face value, and this may well be the last "collective" sentiment shared by everyone here.

The French and the Canadians arrived at Sarajevo airport today to ensure the safe delivery of canned goods to black marketeers. Whatever they don't want is then distributed to honest folk. But these Blue Helmets won't succeed in defending the idea of a "Sarajevo Wall"—which is what the aggressors want to erect here. More precisely, "humanitarian aid" to Sarajevo cannot, by itself, absolve the criminals of what they are doing here and in a thousand other places in Bosnia-Herzegovina. This won't be enough to give them amnesty for the endless tragedy into which they have plummeted our world.

During the last few days we cleaned up the streets and made our parks a little more presentable. We cut down or trimmed all the trees damaged by mortar shells from the hills. There is a bit of electricity, and water, so at least we won't look like complete savages when, one of these days, a peace mission pulls into town—maybe Mitterand's, maybe Carrington's. Surely the venerable gentleman will be pleasantly surprised by the housekeeping we've managed to do since the last visit. Even though times are hard, he'll have his Scotch. We'll even find something for him to eat, although we won't be able to offer him our specialty, grilled *ćevapi.** But after those gestures of hospitality, he'll have to answer our question, "Why did you come?" To again seat the "three sides of the conflict" around the same table? To tell us, "You've gotten your canned goods—so now accept the division of your country"?

That's not a deal we can accept. All these big boxes of food (long past their expiration dates), all the cartons of Marlboros, all the Cokes and chocolate won't do. Lord Carrington must know how many of our brothers and sisters, how many of our best friends, how many brave strangers have died in the last eighty days in the great ghetto consisting of Grbavica, the airport district, and part of Dobrinja. They died because he personally has been supporting certain lunatics in their assertion that this land belongs to them. Does he know how many people have been murdered because various warlords have thought they could get away with things they never got away with before? He does *not* know. And so he'll be just another tourist drinking our beer, enjoying our *ćevapi.* But this is not a time for tourism, and he knows why. We'll survive without canned goods if we have to. Besides, there's nothing in those cans as tasty as the *ćevapi* we hope to cook again one day.

*Traditional Yugoslav meatballs.

KIND PEOPLE

The world is small, and inhabited by kind people. And also, evidently, by a great number of idiots. The difference between them is that the latter find it easy to recognize one another quickly, join up, and stay together. The former occur in small pockets here and there. You have to find them, discover them, let yourself be surprised every time one of them shows up unexpectedly. This may be what renders their existence all the more marvelous, important, and meaningful.

Out of the complete obscurity of despair and loneliness, these great souls emerge. They prove that all is not lost, that we must persevere. They're the ones who find new strength at precisely the moment when despair is about to over-whelm them.

This morning I watched an old woman picking coins out of an old paper bag to pay for a loaf of bread. She was looking to see if she had enough for another loaf. When she realized that she didn't, she turned, with a look of resigna-tion, and started to walk away. The salesperson, a young man in his early twenties, took a loaf out of his basket and put it in the old woman's bag. A man waiting in line rummaged in his pocket, brought out a few coins, and tried to give them to the woman, but she refused. "The bread, that's different, thank you very much, but I can't accept money. I have money of my own, it's just that it isn't enough to buy two loaves every day, for myself and my family. I'm so embarrassed. . . ." Naturally, this is no time for shame. It is another thing altogether, though, to become accustomed to it.

Suad Kovač, an unknown entity until yesterday, has become a benefactor to thousands of Sarajevans. If we had had enough coffee and newspapers to go around, that's all the citizens would have talked about over their coffee and newspapers—about this Suad, a man who had two suitcases full of bank notes, earned in the days when the small business he has with his brother was doing well. He took those two suitcases to the people of Mejtaš, a devastated and famished part of Sarajevo. Those with no income, and those with less than ten thousand dinars a month, were encouraged to get in line to receive some money. Suad wanted to give it only to the most destitute. He wasn't handing it out at random, but according to lists he had drawn up and verified on the basis of a single criterion: who in Mejtaš had money, who didn't.

His "local aid" (his own term) amounted to seventeen thousand dinars. Or seventeen thousand billion dinars, as his elders would say. The oldest among them called it "money from Heaven." At the time I heard the news, more than three hundred people had already gone to the store to buy something with Suad's money—no matter what, as long as it was something to eat.

Today this benefactor has announced that he has money for another five hundred people, and that there will be even more after that. He has also said that he doesn't want any publicity. "I'm not doing this to have people talk about it. I'm doing it to help people, because I have enough. Whenever my brother and I need some more, we'll earn it, as long as we can keep our heads on our shoulders. . . ."

Another thing we'd be reading about over our coffee, if we had newspapers and coffee, is that as of today, Sarajevo's cab drivers will take you anywhere you want for free, and will continue to do so until the war is over. They announced this to the Mayor's office yesterday. I know our cab drivers; they won't find it hard to make up the loss when the time comes.

Someone told me he hailed a cab last night, after nightfall, and asked the driver—fully expecting a refusal—to take him "as close to Dobrinja as you can." The driver floored it and delivered him to the suburb in record time, reminding him to keep his head down. When they arrived, one of our own on the barricades asked the driver what he was doing in this dangerous neighborhood. And the driver simply said, "What the fuck's the difference? This guy isn't joyriding. He must have a reason to come. So I help him."

There are generous human beings in Sarajevo. Their kindness isn't based on misery, but on a sense of what's beautiful.

4 July 1992

THE FLIES AND THE
WEREWOLVES

Here we go again. Lord Carrington arrived, with his entourage. Then he left again. At long last Izetbegović is no longer concerned about hospitality and international largesse. He is concentrating on the cruel reality that is attacking his country. Fiery carpets of shells have once again fallen on the city, and the nocturnal beasts in the hills have tried once again to infiltrate the world of human beings.

The rest is déjà vu. The small white armored vehicles, in considerably greater numbers than before, are showing their "authority" by buzzing around the city like flies around shit. Their carapaces teem with men wearing ridiculous goggles and huge yellow gloves. Under the blue flag, they cruise down avenues strewn with bricks, broken glass, shells, and human suffering. In their seemingly aimless progress, they probably don't even have time to notice the scornful faces of those they have come to protect. And I can well imagine the scorn the "troops" in the hills will feel once they get to spraying these bizarrely attired Blues with sniper fire. This will happen as soon as the Blues have installed themselves in what remains of the Holiday Inn in the heart of the city.

As for yesterday's other events, there's nothing out of the ordinary to report. Radovan Karadžić and his henchmen have renewed their efforts to fool the outside world, and they have been moderately successful. First of all, Karadžić tried to enter Sarajevo in the wake of the UN force, under the protection of the blue flag, to "conduct negotiations" here with the British lord. Even though the latter, living in the rarefied air of aristocracy, doesn't have any idea what is really going on here, he did get cold feet and nixed the meeting. Perhaps someone pointed out to him that a man wanted as a criminal would not be safe in the streets of this city, not even under the protection of the blue flag. After that, Karadžić invited His Lordship to Lukavica and dictated to him his conditions for a cease-fire. Here in Sarajevo we learned that the creature Karadžić would like to transform Bosnia-Herzegovina into a confederation, but that the lord realized this would be impossible. Which is why he told foreign journalists (ours weren't there—they knew very well that once in Lukavica, they would be stabbed to death or become hostages) that it had been a "disappointing afternoon." We're sorry to hear that. But since it looked as if the lord had had a few drinks, I don't understand why he was so disappointed, especially since he didn't even visit our city. Here he might have seen some depressing things, if such things could have any effect on persons of such blue and glacial blood as His Lordship.

The war goes on, in spite of the morsels the world tries to send us to strengthen the black market and fatten the bureaucrats. Common mortals may buy these goods at fluctuating prices. Yesterday, for instance, at the downtown market, a package of survival goods for two days, flown in a few hours earlier by a Hercules transport plane, cost fifty-four thousand dinars. A pack of cigarettes was eighteen hundred dinars for Yorks or twenty-four hundred for Marlboros. People whose names are still on the lists drawn up by state bureaucrats (although it is hard to understand what gives them this authority, since they are to blame for the conditions we live in) receive these packages and cigarettes, with less trouble and for less money, by collecting them at warehouses the bureaucrats have established so that "things won't get out of control."

Not much to report from Sarajevo. Once again they've attacked the ruins of the *Oslobodenje* building (although the paper keeps coming out) with all kinds of armaments, and this time even with foot soldiers. We exchanged some invective a little before dawn, in the fading dark. Being afraid of light, like all werewolves, they then faded away. It is incredible to see how vulnerable they are to daylight.

The weather is fine, sunny and hot. This morning the mark was worth more than two thousand dinars (it's still difficult to figure out *which* dinars), and a kilo of potatoes costs four marks. We keep going, waiting for the night and another encounter with werewolves. There will be moonlight. They will come.

5 July 1992

THE YELLOW HIGH RISE

In the ninety days that this unbelievable war in Bosnia-Herzegovina and the siege of Sarajevo has lasted, we've seen just about everything. But what could be seen with the naked eye, what could be watched like a soccer match, a movie, or the circus, at number 21 of what we now call Blood Givers Street, must surpass every imaginable violation of internationally sanctioned conventions.

Twenty minutes of artillery fire poured onto a large residential complex in the heart of the city. The attack that came on this sunny July day, only a few hundred kilometers from Rome, Venice, Florence, Paris, Vienna, or Athens, makes any further talk of international order unneccesary. What makes the whole thing even more overwhelming—for the refined world that only acknowledges in wartime what can be seen or proven, like photos or substantial testimony—TV cameras recorded and televised the pounding taken by this huge yellow building, from start to finish.

Military experts already know that a "member of one of the sides involved in the conflict" (as various observers of the aggression directed against Bosnia-Herzegovina never tire of saying, including some *very* foreign journalists) opened fire on the building with a forty-millimeter antiaircraft gun. They also know that there are fifty-six holes left in the facade of the high rise, not counting the damage caused by projectiles entering apartments directly through windows. Only the survivors among the tenants of the building—who will stay alive, no doubt, as yet another symbol of Sarajevo's unbelievability—also know that not a single apartment between the tenth and the eighteenth floor was spared.

The shots fired from the weapon, the holes it left behind, and the smoke billowing from the destroyed facade—we've seen this a thousand times here in Sarajevo. But the way it was carried out this time, on Blood Givers Street, probably has never been seen before. The maniac sitting behind the gun did his work in such a clear and determined way that nothing remains to be said. He began his feast of blood coolly and slowly, with a few random bursts, then zeroed in with diabolical precision, starting with the eighteenth floor and lowering his aim systematically, floor by floor, window by window, apartment by apartment, wall by wall. He did it with sadistic slowness, giving the people in the building just enough time between bursts to hope that the attack might be over, that they would be spared.

In this supposed heartland of Europe, that forty-millimeter gun has calmly and with an idiot's arrogance expressed everything those people wish to tell the rest of the planet: "As far as the question of shooting goes, here it is, from A to Z. Yes, we're shooting—so what? Take your 'civilization' and shove it. Everyone here knows who is master of life and death. This shot is for your conference tables and resolutions! This shot is for your Blue Helmets and other scum! And this shot is for everyone with the nerve to say what we can or cannot do!"

Each of the fifty-six holes in the front of the building counted by the naked eye is a huge red hole in the so-called order of things we think exists. Apparently the victory of evil continues on unabated—the powerlessness of good, the triumph of chaos over order, the verification of defeat in the match between humanity and the bestial goes on.

There is a feeling of impotence and endless sorrow as that which "couldn't happen anywhere in the world" takes place before your very eyes. An animal sits behind a gun giggling sadistically, and slowly, with great measure and endless pleasure, he chooses window by window whether to kill one, two, five, or however many people he wants. Why did we think this "couldn't happen anywhere in the world"? Why were we taught that there is an order to things on this terrestrial sphere? And why has this happened now? Because the "order of things" was buried in Sarajevo. It is the grandest and saddest funeral that has taken place on this planet in decades. Not because of the number of victims, but for the enormity of a whole mountain of irredeemably buried ideals.

To top it off, in the story of the yellow high rise there is one thing that, while unimportant for that maniac, is decisive for us. From out of the huge pile of bricks, concrete, glass, and steel left after the shelling, a ten-day-old baby was pulled, alive and well. Alive to remember what they'll tell her about her tenth day, well enough to transform that memory into what she thinks worthwhile—so that the story of this yellow high rise will never again have to be told. Only insofar, of course, as she, that baby, does not sink into the existing "order."

6 July 1992

THE "LIBERATION" OF GRBAVICA

Radovan Karadžić, a fascist compared to whom any former SS man is an epic hero from a children's story, is not wasting a second in carrying out his monstrous "cleansing" project in territories he has proclaimed to be his, accompanied by remarkable indifference not only from members of the international community, but even from people living only a few hundred kilometers from this inferno. Three days ago this monster declared to the world, amongst a series of other incredible statements, that he will "open the borders for three days, so that the Serbs are free to leave the Muslim part of Sarajevo and go where they wish, and the same option will be available to all the others." Once again, this terrorist-political creature has demonstrated, as always, that he is truly ready to honor his promises.

Yesterday and today, first singly, but then in ever-increasing numbers, across bridges that formerly linked the two banks of the Miljacka but that now make them seem infinitely distant from one another, Muslims and Croats have been seeking refuge in this, the free side of Sarajevo. Except for a few bundles in their hands, they left everything they had behind, just to get out with their heads on their shoulders. They've also brought with them terrifying stories, virtually unbelievable when put in the context of this place and time. Indeed, every story that shocks Sarajevo today, aside from the fact that they are so horrible in themselves, has with it this added shock: that they have happened here, and are transpiring now.

For the Muslims, Croats, and "disobedient" Serbs, Grbavica is a ghetto in the true sense of the word. It is actually worse than a ghetto; Grbavica is a concentration camp. At first the torture was limited to nocturnal raids by idiots in stocking masks who came down off the slopes of Trebević only to go back up there to their caves before the first rays of the sun. Then they proceeded to capture house by house, one quarter after another, not permitting the inhabitants of these captured houses to "move around unnecessarily." Then they broke through to the bank of the Miljacka and dug themselves in, completely closing the circle around those who had stayed in Grbavica—either because they couldn't believe that it had come to this, or simply because they didn't want to leave what was theirs and everything they had strived for over decades.

After that, only "obedient" Serbs had permission to go out into the street during the day to buy whatever was left to be had. The story resumes with the persecution of every Serb who didn't answer the call for mobilization into the "Serbian Army," and the implementation of a concentration camp regimen for Muslims and Croats. Enforced "work duty" meant that they were ordered to perform daily physical labor, to dig trenches, build barricades, or clean the streets under the supervision of armed guards.

The next step was predictable; transports began, en

masse and in trucks, and many have not been heard from since. The most courageous, or those whose nerves were clearly shattered, turned their anguish into an attempted escape across the river. The monsters opened fire on them, and later installed submerged high-tension cables. With this, the story marches to its end.

People who had stopped believing in any possibility of getting out were suddenly given permission to leave. Before the eyes of the world, Mr. Karadžić has "kept his promise." He has "let go" all those who wanted "out." He has achieved a goal he hasn't been able to reach in Sarajevo, as he already has along the Drina: butchering and mangling everything that is not Serb. Grbavica is now his domain, and I'm sure he'll think of something for those who still don't want to leave, who don't want "out," some appropriate manner to appear "humane and democratic," just the way the inventors of the theory of the "conflicting parties in Sarajevo" would like.

BOSNIAN STOMACH TROUBLE

It's a long, humid, ordinary, monotonous, even boring summer day. No distractions whatsoever. People meeting in the street scarcely ask each other anything anymore. Imagine reaching a point at which it seems stupid to inquire: "How is it going?" "Are you alive?" "How's the family?" Now a nod in passing suffices, and everyone goes on coping with his or her own troubles. Speaking of which, one can't help envying those with tough nerves, the ones who haven't lost their sense of humor and manage to pursue some kind of activity, besides survival. In an odd but quite discernible way, these are the people who keep the city from falling apart. They hold their heads above water, just high enough to keep afloat, until some new ship appears, bearing a new cargo of bottled optimism and compressed internal strength.

Three news items, however, distinguish today from yesterday:

There are no more jostling crowds in front of the district offices in which our militant social realists are enjoying their second youth, bent over lists of American aid and stacks of ration cards, their spectacles balanced on their noses, chewing erasers, as they show great satisfaction at the word "comrade" coming back into fashion as a mode of address. They have made a forceful comeback on the municipal scene, and they have no trouble at all being accepted as the new managers of the small plastic packets labeled "beef stew," "chicken and rice," "ham slice with natural juice," "sherry nut cake." . . .

In the early morning the telephones (a rare commodity) of the municipal offices are used to find someone who could translate the instructions on a brown plastic bag containing an unindentifiable substance, neither liquid nor solid nor gaseous, labeled "beef stew." More perceptive office workers conclude that there is no way a packet that small could contain ten *ćevapi* in a thick pita with lots of onions, and "to hell with *ćevapi* that can't be wolfed down on the spot." The American magic encapsulated in plastic and cardboard proved disillusioning, as did the fact that there wasn't "a drop of beer" in the parcels. The packets of ersatz instant coffee were no good, not even for making a cup of tea, not to mention a cup of good black Turkish coffee in a *fildjan*.

Nevertheless, people kept transporting, and translating. And eating, of course. Luckily, we still had enough bread of our own left, which, against the American "spaghetti with meat sauce," won hands down.

There isn't much to the second item. Again, they kept firing at our newspaper building all night, and this morning they succeeded in setting fire to the part that housed the large work spaces, the dispensary, the post office, and the big cafeteria we used to call the "skin restaurant." Snipers killed a man at the entrance, then spent the morning preventing the fire brigade from extinguishing the fire. A detachment of more than seven hundred Canadians of the UN Protection Force was stationed, literally, less than a hundred yards away from the conflagration. The commander of the barracks housing these Blues told us, not without some agitation, that the "makeup men" had been sent out immediately to the burning *Oslobodenje* building to inquire, "Have soldiers belonging to the army of Alija Izetbegović taken part in this assault?" After examining our rocket launchers and mortars, they went to lunch. Their choice of beverages included milk, coffee, hot chocolate, or tea with lemon. Then there was cheese, ham, and butter, followed by a rare steak with a lettuce and tomato salad, and chocolate mousse or pudding for dessert. They invited us to share their lunch with them. I told them thanks, but no thanks. "But why not?" they wanted to know. "Summer's coming—have to slim down for the beach," I told them, keeping a straight face, and they accepted my excuse, looking equally imperturbable.

The third item is a little oddity: I saw a watchmaker's shop that was open for business. What struck me as odd was not that shops are still open, but that there still are people here who are interested in knowing what time it is, and that there are other people who might actually know.

Unimportant news: The ferocious barrage continues.

11 July 1992

CITY AROUND THE CORNER

Along with a quantity of foodstuffs and beverages absolutely beyond belief in these times—not to mention the quality of this food, brought in via a VW from Split—I have new guests, Boris, a reporter, and Željko, a photojournalist, both from the Split daily *Slobodna Dalmacija*. Just before merry midnight, and with completely straight faces, they told me, "Tomorrow you'll have to do your best to convince us that the war here really is everything you've made it out to be. . . ."

A few hours later, in the morning, we managed to survive by the skin of our teeth. First, we dodged the bullets of a sniper who had us in his sights. And then, right afterward, we were almost hit by a car careening out of control, its driver a victim of the same devil behind the telescopic sight. After driving across town to *Oslobodenje*, our impressions were complete. We were jolted quickly and brutally back into a reality that simply is what it is.

The entire population seems to have lodged itself at street corners, near intersections. Your first thought is that people are just hanging out there from morning till night; then you realize that these are, in fact, the same people you saw yesterday. Their faces are the same, their apprehensive glances at the sniper-infested hills are the same, even their hesitant stance is the same; is this the right moment to venture out into the street to play Russian roulette?

Instead of firing mortar shells, which are now most frequently reserved for the night, the animals from the hills spend the day controlling every intersection in the city. They take obvious pleasure in a bloody game whose object is to stop the few city buses that have begun running once again the last few days, trying to create an illusion of the better days Sarajevo anticipates.

It is difficult to comprehend how the *chetniks* are capable of doing what they're doing with sniper fire. What kind of mentality enables a person to sit down in a stolen armchair on one of those wooded slopes that offers a perfect view of the streets of Sarajevo, place a box of dum-dum ammunition and the obligatory bottle of tepid slivovitz next to the chair, and then proceed to scan the streets for victims? The distance is too great to distinguish between young and old, men, women, or children. Nationality is obviously beside the point. The point is to aim at the head, shoot to kill, and pull the trigger two or three times while the victim is caught in the telescopic sight. Yesterday the snipers scored several bull's eyes: four dead, ten wounded. The buses had to change their routes, but the life of the people lurking at the street corners goes on.

People no longer tell each other where they happened to find themselves under fire, they're no longer curious about who has been hit. It's all become just a matter of bad luck. Nevertheless, it wouldn't dawn on anyone not to go on their way, moving about this or that part of the city. You have to keep believing that it won't happen to you. "These things happen only to others"—that theory must remain in force to the end. Once it weakens, it is no longer even a theory, it is nothing.

But as Enko Mehmedbašić writes in our daily paper, reality doesn't seem interesting to anyone except to those contemplating suicide. That, at least, has become easy, and exacts much less pain than other, voluntary methods of curtailing life; all you need to do is to stop in the middle of one of Sarajevo's intersections and stay there. It doesn't matter which way you're looking—it won't take long. Death will come quickly and without warning.

It's hard to tell whether this notion of "suicide Sarajevo-style" restores the city to its splendid tradition of gallows humor, or whether it is simply a question of the grim truth itself. Not that it matters, but there is good reason for either to be true.

12 July 1992

AN ENCOUNTER WITH
THE FUTURE

A routine two-hour visit to the Koševo Hospital sums up the experience of the war in Sarajevo. Thousands of individual dramas are condensed into one desperate convulsion in an attempt to survive; then, after that, who knows?

Last night the orthopedic ward was under fire. A shell crashed through six rooms, leaving devastation in its wake. Scattered in the corners of the rooms lie abandoned crutches, which the patients had been clutching at like straws, in the hope that one day they could walk again. Overturned beds, blood, cement . . . If he survives, Bešlija Jazmir, a soldier from the front, will remember his fractured femur as an insignificant episode compared to the stomach wounds he received here last night. On the outside wall of the building, the shell's entry hole is surprisingly small, not crater-shaped at all; once inside, piercing one wall after another, the shell caused increasing damage, and sought out the same unlucky ones who had already been wounded in the bloody episode of Vasa Miskin Street. Death came for them a second time.

The first time they said it was a mine; today Srna Television (Sarajevo's Serb television station) will claim in one of its outrageously laughable broadcasts that "the hospital was attacked by Alija's soldiers in order to deceive the world once again—to make it appear that Sarajevo is being bombarded by Serbs, while in reality we stand for peace and favor a political solution." Boris Dežulović, a writer for *Slobodna Dalmacija*'s satirical supplement *Feral Tribune*, comments that *Feral* became obsolete as soon as Srna began broadcasting. The station has become a cornucopia of cynical humor, lies, and absurdities, outdoing any competitor worldwide.

But the story of the hospital is also the story of the children on the second floor of the orthopedic ward, among whom there are those who have had an arm or a leg amputated and are already showing a subconscious desire to prove themselves faster and more agile on their crutches than others. On the surface they seem in good spirits and extraordinarily willing and able to tell you how, where, and why they became forever different from other children in the world. But they're already fighting their personal battles with sleepless nights and the emotional traumas they carry like a brand displaying their difference from others. One of them had been carrying ammunition to Trebević. (Whose idea was that, and why?) Another had simply been playing in the wrong place, providing a target for a sniper. A third had been standing too close to a window when one of those flying "mines" landed.

In the hallway of the ward where these children begin their new lives as mutilated, amputated, permanently handicapped people, one may see vestiges of another time, remnants of other habits: large posters of the Pink Panther, Asterix the Gaul, and Donald Duck. Who in this clinic today, without a leg or a hand, wonders who the Pink

Panther is, where that Duck is, or where Asterix comes from? But they will know, for the rest of their lives, who Dr. Karadžić is, they will learn about the monster Mladić, and Ostajić the criminal, and Milošević, Ćosić, Bulatović, and the rest. . . . They will also know who we are, we who didn't know early enough how to protect their childhood, their legs or their hands. And they will also know what to think of a world that mumbles on about justice, order, and truth, of law, responsibility, and continuity.

There may be some who think that a four-month-old baby who has just had a leg amputated will never try to find out why she was "born" without a leg and why others were not. Does anyone really think that there can be an adequate answer to such a question? And does anyone truly believe that the absence of an adequate answer can mean anything but the beginning of a search for the truth, a truth demanded as an elementary right to leading a free life? May the mothers lament all of us who are left, in the years to come, as we face today's children without legs or hands, in the anguish of Sarajevo's orthopedic clinic, and who knows how many other orthopedic, pediatric surgery, and trauma wards in hospitals throughout Bosnia-Herzegovina and its surroundings. Not to mention those children who never had a chance to be taken to a hospital.

The hospital is an excellent place for an encounter with the future. May God help us, and these children in the hospitals.

13 July 1992

ONE HUNDRED DAYS OF SOLITUDE

Today, according to our calculations, is an anniversary: one hundred days of solitude. It has been exactly a hundred days since the first shot was fired on a citizen of Sarajevo, when a sniper killed a young girl who was walking across a bridge. Until that day, the bridge was simply a way of crossing a river we shared. Since then, it has become a border, the sign of intolerable division.

I don't know how everyone will remember these hundred days, during which everything has turned upside down, and after which nothing will ever be the same again. It's hard to say whether anyone will really want to remember at all. Among other things, now isn't quite the time for remembering; it is, perhaps, a moment to have a close look at what we are today, and what we once were but are no longer.

We no longer live in the same places, we don't have the same neighbors, we no longer speak the same language, and we don't know each other the way we once did. We no longer go to the same bakery or the same newsstand. The hinges of entrance gates no longer squeak the same way, the birds who used to feed off our palms no longer alight on our balconies. Our relatives are no longer buried in the same cemeteries, and we are unable to visit the graves of those who went before them. Who knows if those graves are still there?

We no longer switch the light on in our apartments; no longer use our dinner dishes; the piles of plastic water buckets in the hallways and under our beds (if we still have a bed) no longer bother us. We've forgotten what it was like to be irritated by a television commercial. We don't get angry at the mailman for coming late, because there no longer is a mailman. We would give anything in the world just to get a bill, no matter how big or how small, because it would mean that someone believes we're still alive and capable of paying.

And people have changed. Laughter and tears come in waves, even out of place, uncontrolled, like a hysterical complaint. At times they flow despite clenched jaws. No one minds.

The worst of it is that we have learned to hate. We have become suspicious, and don't trust anyone. We no longer know how to hope. We've become cynical and scornful. Someone told me recently that Bosnians have reached a point beyond hatred. There are times when you are ready to pack it in and leave, if only you could, but we've retained something quite essential—a nastiness, out of spite, if you will, or plain stupidity, that makes it easier for others to recognize us. This is what keeps us here and will probably cost a lot of us our heads. But what good is a head if its boundaries are set by idiots from the back hills? If there is no space left in it for an ornery remnant?

A hundred days is nothing. A spring we haven't seen, a winter that is constantly upon us. Nevertheless, these hundred days are engraved in our memories as if they had been a hundred years. Of a solitude with and within ourselves, in a convulsive attempt to learn a way of life we have never known. How to get across that wall, as in *Jonathan Livingston Seagull*, how to gain the speed and altitude that would allow us to escape this solitude? Even if only to find another kind of solitude outside the ring of steel dreamt up by non-people to dominate people. Selim, my greengrocer, thought we had a chance. He is no longer with us. Boro, the waiter at the corner café, and Dario at the newsstand, both used to say the same thing. Both of them are gone. As is the big oak tree in the park across the street: people with foresight are already cutting off its branches to use as fuel in the winter. What winter? It is already winter, when winter is all around us.

14 July 1992

A LONG HOT SUMMER

I walked all the way across town today, from the cathedral to *Oslobodenje*, down streets where everything seemed to be as it was in the old days. Lots of people, open sidewalk cafés, children playing, mothers calling for them. I also saw streets from another, completely desolate, planet; sidewalks overgrown with weeds, overturned and charred automobiles, burned buildings, dogs rooting through piles of garbage.

Then I reached the Holiday Inn. Getting inside isn't that easy, because the snipers take a shot at everything that moves. But once you're inside it's easy to forget what's happening outside. Since the glass walls of the National restaurant face the Hills of Death, food is now served in the former conference hall. Everything else—the reception desk, the foyer, the bar—looks just as it did six months ago. In the restaurant the tables are laid with immaculate white tablecloths. The silver cutlery and the water and wine glasses are sparkling. Everything is perfect. The waiters look as if they had no inkling of what goes on outside. The menu offers steaks, french fries, beef stew, crêpes with chocolate sauce. The waiter, cool as ever, leaves—to the horror of the diner—a few french fries on the serving tray and is about to take them back to the kitchen. I don't know if this is a matter of etiquette, a custom from the past, or whether a friend of his is waiting for him behind the kitchen door, ready to pounce on leftovers.

Downstairs, in the foyer, a notice board gives details of the program for the group that will arrive by air from Belgrade at half past eleven. Their guide is Saduko Ogata from the United Nations Refugee Commission, or the UNHCR. The group will first visit a refugee center, then proceed to the President's building, briefly, and finally to where they had originally set out for: Lukavica, where they'll meet with Radovan Karadžić. Yes, that's exactly what it says on the board: "Lukavica—Mr. Karadžić." Later they'll meet Radovan's buddies at the UNPROFOR headquarters, and then fly back to Belgrade. That will have been their mission to Sarajevo.

I must admit that I felt faint when I saw, in black and white, on a notice board in the center of Sarajevo, that certain gentlemen have arranged a meeting with a criminal who has thrown the operation of this very hotel into disarray, who has killed people who have stayed in it, and who is personally responsible for demolishing the side of the hotel that faces the hills. What kind of tolerance is it that makes this possible, what kind of idiocy allows Radovan Karadžić to be included in a sightseeing tour of Sarajevo, a city now noted with interest for its destruction and devastation, for its brand-new ruins? Isn't it just charming to go on a trip to such an exotic zoo, to such a nature preserve?

Yesterday the gentlemen from UNPROFOR earned another merit badge in the eyes of Sarajevo's citizens. In one of their snow-white official vehicles, accompanied by two equally white armored cars, the boys of the HVO (The

Croat Defence Council) found a notorious *chetnik* being given a ride from one barrack to another, no doubt to accomplish a special mission. Richard Grey, the Blue colonel, almost died of fright when he and his men were pulled out of the car, and journalists were summoned to witness and photograph the event. But so what? These fellows driving around in their white tin cans have really become a laughingstock to be whistled at. And yet we pinned so many hopes on them at first. . . .

Days in Sarajevo flow on and on like this. Some young men worth their weight in gold have been mobilized and given rifles to carry. It was no longer possible for them to continue whatever it was they were doing before, which was probably a thousand times more important than carrying a rifle. Others, those with connections, still sit in the cafés, ruminating. Street intersections can still be lethal. Certain Sarajevans are beginning to receive parcels from the wounded city of Zadar. As long as there are people, we'll survive. Survival is even helped along by the presence of a few idiots; it keeps things from getting too monotonous. Our captured colleague, Memica Husić, has been freed in an exchange. A nest of machine guns that had been firing at *Oslobodenje* for weeks has been destroyed. There are fewer and fewer telephones in working order, and we hear that Bush is going on vacation. It'll be a long, hot summer.

THE GAME OF ABSURDITY

How to speak of the general situation in Sarajevo on the day of the death of a friend and colleague, a photojournalist, a great pro? When, to boot, you learn that somewhere on the other side of the Miljacka, in "Serb Sarajevo," another dear man, from the same company, has died because he could no longer bear the fear and the famine? And, finally, on a day when, with your own eyes, you have just seen a six-month-old baby whose leg was amputated an hour or two ago?

How to describe the sensation of things closing in on you, slowly but surely? It's as if you are standing in line, and the line is moving forward, and in the end you arrive at this ticket window where you have to pay for everything that had till now been priceless: love, happiness, intimacy, mad faith in people and humanity, trust, and generosity.

And it is on a day like this that I welcome in my office (where I go every day, past a wall behind which a sniper waits for me) a German TV journalist with his cameramen. His first question: "What is your reaction to General MacKenzie's statement that the people of Sarajevo are not appreciative of the food the Blue Helmets have ensured by their airlift?"

Indeed, why aren't we (I say we because I include myself

among the ingrates), when it is clear that a few warehouses are bulging with supplies of flour, macaroni, and rice?

What is the cause of this ingratitude, considering that now only a few children get killed every day, instead of the many more that had been getting killed before? Why are we ungrateful, now that we have the chance to leave the city with the Blue Helmets, provided we can come up with a nice round sum? Can't we buy gasoline from them if we want to, if we can afford the price? Or find out gratis through their intermediaries that those who killed my friend Salko Honda, the photojournalist, will never be brought to justice?

I keep my cool and don't tell the man from German TV that my spontaneous response to his even asking me such a question would be a howl of rage; that I can only shed tears of pain over the "valuable" TV news that reports about how "UNPROFOR has brought devices to Sarajevo to enable them to identify the nature and provenance of the shots fired," but that there is nobody I can ask about that child's amputated leg, or about my friend Salko, who, only a year away from retirement, trembled with fear at the shelling, before falling victim to a shell himself.

In short, our situation is becoming absurd. Absurd because, while we once had hope, we remain where we are, separated from our nearest and dearest. Absurd because we believed that anyone would do anything to help us. Absurd because we didn't understand that General MacKenzie (who will soon take leave of Sarajevo) never intended to do more than arrive here, dabble for a bit, sew another star on his uniform (woven from the blood of Sarajevo's children), then go back to his Canadian lakes.

But it is precisely because of this, because of this absurdity, because of Salko Honda who died camera in hand, because of little Rade who couldn't bear the hunger and fear (which was understandable), because of my children who are growing up with no father around, that we can shake hands with the absurd, and mock it, cheat it, steal from it, just as it does to us. Now all that's left is the absurd, and us. In this rotten world so much has been turned upside down that we have to place our bets on the impossible. Only in a joust with the absurd can we find a shred of sense.

The people here are bitter but honest. Since they're honest, they must be crazy. And since they're crazy, they think a fight with the absurd is possible. They hope that they have a chance to win. That's the point we've come to.

THE LIONS IN THE LION CEMETERY

It's 2:00 P.M., and no one has been killed yet. It is a strange, torrid July afternoon. Because no one has been killed yet, because the firing is distant, it has been possible to bury those who were killed yesterday and the day before, as well as those whose corpses have lain for days in the dark and cold of hospital rooms serving as morgues. Processions of silent, exhausted, anxious people have made their way to the old Lion Cemetery, which has been reopened by a special decree from the municipal authorities.

Located between a shaded avenue that leads to Koševo Stadium and a quiet street next to the Trauma Center, this cemetery has not seen many visitors lately. It is named after a monumental sculpture of a lion with a royal mane. Now it has become the only meeting place for Sarajevans who don't have any other occasion for gathering in large numbers in the same place.

Slowly at first, then more rapidly every day, a yellow wave of freshly turned soil replaces what was an untended lawn under the lion's paws. This wave spreads in all directions and devours parts of the cemetery that had already been sold for other uses. Two, three, ten, fifteen burials a day is the Sarajevan rhythm of passage from life to death.

All the many years of life in Sarajevo, and for Sarajevo, can be seen in the shade of the Lion's Graveyard, as revealing as the palm of your hand. Sarajevo is really just a small town; it has great soul, and everyone here knows everyone else. These folk are the only ones buried here, beside the concrete lion, whose mane has long been well chewed. But those who, for now, have found their resting place in the grass courtyards of Dobrinja, and in other places where the dead could not be carried out for a decent funeral, one day they will be here. The Lion's graves are the final resting places for those who are truly of Sarajevo, who refused to leave, and so will remain here forever.

It is astonishing to note that you recognize practically all the names on the hundreds and hundreds of inscriptions, even though some have faded; it is stupefying to see the names of people you had met only days before, smiling and convinced that you would meet again in the future. Then you realize that death in this city comes silently, unannounced, leaving not even the minimal space necessary for the farewell that befits us. Under the dense foliage of the cemetery trees, you find the names of people you grew up with and knew in high school, names of others with whom you dreamed of your first journeys abroad, great journeys to happiness, to the infinite. We recognize the names of those with whom we lost touch, and only now, here, do we understand that we've always been members of the same Sarajevo band, that we loved the same life, that we dug ourselves the same grave because we didn't know how, or didn't want, to defy the hicks from the woods when we should have. We just kept telling jokes at their expense, while they came down from the hills, dragging one after another, hating us because we knew about soap and water, about washing our feet and wearing clean socks. So we congregate here today below the Lion, the lucky ones who are still standing and those of our gang who found themselves at the wrong place at the wrong time, and now lie here side by side.

There isn't a graveyard anywhere in the world quite like the Lion. Here are hundreds and hundreds of people who probably never knew each other, but who belonged to the great family of regular people, people who looked to the future and weren't crazed by their genes, or by the phony myths about their past; people who weren't trapped inside a tight flock where survival can only be collective and ruled by the authority of a Leader and the blood oath.

By the feet of the stone Lion are other lions who have something exceptional in common: the same year of departure, the year of the bloodbath—1992. It took some of them young, some of them older. May it be cursed, this year 1992, for driving six feet underground people who loved people. Who will pay, and when, and how, for the new inscriptions to be carved on the markers of these fresh graves? These are the freshest, all lined up in rows. They will have to be paid for. And the price, I guarantee you, won't be cheap.

21 July 1992

DENIAL OF A MANDATE
FOR LIFE

A strange tension has spread through the city. Everybody's nervous and impatient. It is becoming clearer and clearer that Sarajevo is caught in a lassitude that could continue a long time, perhaps a very long time. No reason for hope, no solution in sight. And they continue to kill us, one by one. The only thing that grows is the Cemetery of the Lion. Even the last, most intimate stratum of expectations that something significant will happen has been buried in the very depths of the soul. The airport has been closed again. Yesterday we all saw a convoy of tanks and armored vehicles with *chetnik* flags cross the runway. The convoys bringing humanitarian aid have been stopped at Split and at Kiseljak. The Blues senselessly bureaucratize when as much as a pin tries to cross their lines into town, endlessly blathering about "mandates" and "procedures," while the *chetniks* receive their arms with neither mandate nor procedure.

We asked some French journalists to send us a few bulletproof vests (since this is a place where journalists are shot at), and they sent them. These vests are now being held in Split, where the *chetniks* and the UNPROFOR won't release them. It isn't hard to understand why the former don't want us to have them, but the latter? What "political imbalance" could result from a few journalists being able to protect their backs and chests from bullets and shrapnel?

We have asked the world to send us newsprint, to keep the paper from dying. It is the only newspaper left in our besieged city. We've been told that newsprint does not belong to the category of humanitarian aid, which is the only category the Blues have been authorized to guarantee.

We have asked for some food, because we often aren't given what has arrived, and if we do get it—a little flour and rice—it doesn't give us enough energy to keep writing, dodging bullets, and putting out fires. There are some good people who've already gathered some food for us, but the international guards at the gates to the city have not received a "mandate" to let them pass. Maybe, they tell us, when the blockade is lifted and the shooting stops. Good God, are they simply being impertinent, numb, or corrupt, or have they really been given a "mandate" to steer our history in the direction of Palestine, Cyprus, and the other countries that have been inundated with noble declarations against partition, genocide, and exodus, though they actually still remain exactly where they were when the guns finished their jobs?

A shell here, a bullet there, a tank in the evening, a sniper in the morning. One life less by one life less, day by day, fall, then winter. This will be, no doubt, a long, cold winter in which everything that was once human in our town will be buried. People who used to live on laughter, good deeds, love, and forgiveness will die. The raw figures built from hatred and sadism will remain, lustfully nourished by the sorrow of others. On the other side of borders made impermeable by UNPROFOR, which the *chetniks* have held with the help of America and Europe, the East and the West, Teheran and the Vatican, electricians and macrobiotics, tons of food will remain—along with paper, antennas, telephones, toys and games, batteries and cassettes that weren't allowed in to help a civilization survive.

It has taken a lot for us to realize why we've been made into sacrificial animals. Because somebody somewhere decided that the bestial concept of a herd composed of only one color, all speaking the same language, all thinking along similar lines, all believing in the same god, must wipe out everything else. They are dangerous, truly dangerous, these people who can use three different words for the same object, who know how to love without asking for a surname, and who can be satisfied in either the sun or the snow. We have not been given a "mandate" to survive. Forget about the "mandate" to bring a pin or a tomato into our city. We have no "mandate" to present our case to the world in the great debate—which is already settled, somewhere out there, by someone unable to abide the mad beauty of different races and mingling genes. That's what this is all about. That's why it is ridiculous to expect anything from the world outside. Everything we need, and can muster for the final battle, is worth searching for, and can only be found within ourselves. No matter the cost.

SMART BOSNIANS AND DUMB BOSNIANS

In Sarajevo this morning, naturally, there's nothing new to report: a little electricity, no water, the usual deaths (ten or so), a carton of eggs (twenty-five German marks), a kilo of pork (fifteen marks). Representatives of three national parties are on their way to London to negotiate our fate. My friend Jovan Divjak, second in command of the army of Bosnia-Herzegovina, tells me, "I'm doing all I can to fight this war, but I'm hardly in Bosnia anymore. In London, the Serbs are represented by Radovan Karadžić—the man whom I am fighting. And I'm neither a Muslim nor a Croat. What a life!"

Avdo Sidran, living legend of Sarajevo, and considered the greatest poet of Bosnia-Herzegovina, has contributed a little poem, which has already been recited all over town today, wherever it is possible to have a drink between mortar shells (a beer—one mark):

Ceasefire

Is it signed?
Of course they signed it.
Has it been broken?
Of course it's been broken.

So what should we do?
We should sign it, God willing.
Just to break it?
Of course just to break it.
For how much longer, damn it?
Till we're all smashed to smithereens,
For the fuck of it.

Our tribulations seem to subside only when we run into Sidran and others like him. I'm not counting, of course, those rare times when we have water. We know practically every millimeter of the city, where you can or cannot cross, where you have to duck, where you have to crawl. We have precisely marked the points where people curse the *chetniks*, or where the UNPROFOR is the subject of derision, or our domestic local political geniuses get it. Of course, the worst politicians are the only ones who are still here. As for those who have left—on some terribly urgent government business—they are refered to, indirectly, in this popular joke: Do you know the difference between a smart Bosnian and a dumb Bosnian? The smart one calls the dumb one every day. From abroad.

Unkind, to be sure. Regrettably, there are more and more of us who don't see this as a joke any more, but still keep on hoping; it's hard to know for what. Perhaps we believe that the negotiations in London or elsewhere may turn out well, and that Karadžić will say, "Gentlemen, may I please be excused? We're all done now, we've finished."

Till then, we stand behind lowered blinds and camou-flaged windows, and look out into the starry summer night sky crisscrossed by the flaming red missiles that rise from both sides of the horizon. As they fall toward the ground they carry off another person's life, curtailing his or her already barren hopes, or perhaps only destroying something built and strived for over a whole lifetime, or longer. The fireworks go on late into the night, sometimes until dawn.

Sleep becomes increasingly difficult, while the number of nocturnal observers multiplies. Now even those down below, on the dark sidewalks and in improvised sentry boxes, no longer have to shout, "Put that out before I shoot it out!" Why bother? Here everything has been extinguished already, and everything is in the dark.

As for the joke about the smart Bosnians, it doesn't even really work anymore, since the division will be a bit more brutal: only the smart ones will be left, since the others will no longer exist. We'll see who cracks jokes about that. No doubt someone will.

30 July 1992

LORD, VICTIMS, AND ZOMBIES

Another shell, right in front of the presidency building; they're shelling the Old Town, Dobrinja, Nedžarići, and the city center. The snipers have become even more despicable: they've started using silencers and dum-dum bullets. Is there any sense in pointing out that these are illegal? That would be ridiculous: what does "legal" mean in this war? The worst of it is that now even our own radio announcer declares that the day has been "relatively" calm. In other words, it is relatively normal to be at war, with at least ten people killed daily, and no one doing anything to stop it. Why no one stops it is becoming clearer and clearer. Here's how:

This morning I went to the office of the local collective (which, by the way, works very well compared to most of the others in the city) to pick up a new packet of humanitarian aid, my second since the beginning of the war. The bag, for which I paid three hundred dinars, contained a can of Irish tuna with a Greek label, a kilo and a half of flour, one hundred grams of powdered milk, one hundred grams of protein-enriched "Oxford biscuit" (with a detailed listing of its calories and protein content), and a box of Danish feta cheese packaged and sold in Iran. Because of this we made a proper little feast in the home that four of us share.

That aid package has to last until the next one, that is to say, God knows how long. Well-informed people claim that 6.5 percent of Sarajevans have been able to "supplement" their diet with such aid. No one even mentions the people in other cities who still haven't received any aid at all. The four of us in my apartment certainly won't die of starvation, because we belong to those who, one way or another, manage to find extra food. And then, who knows, perhaps the HVO (The Croat Defense Council) and the SDS (Serb Democrat Party) will reach an agreement in Stip, and we may be able to get to parcels that have been sent to us by some good people in Dalmatia, Zagreb, Kiseljak, and even France.

The problem, however, is not food. The problem is to learn the real reason for all this commotion about the airport, for all these planes that probably cost a fortune; what good are these bags of flour, tuna, and Oxford biscuits when all the sweet cherries and ripe strawberries from this spring—that used to come to the Sarajevo markets—have rotted in the surrounding fields, thanks to a few hundred bearded assholes posted behind barricades on the roads leading out of the city?

Does anyone really believe it would be a problem to remove these barricades and let Sarajevo buy, transport, deliver, sell, provide, and feed mouths and factories, guarantee wages and production? That has never been the problem, nor is it now. Someone simply doesn't want it to happen. This parade of airplanes and these spoonfuls of protein are convenient for someone, just as the total, crippling blockade of Sarajevo meets someone's needs—

probably to bring about what Carrington said: "Once they're all exhausted, they'll negotiate." The only thing wrong with Lord Carrington's theory is that this war exhausts only one of the parties—the victimized one. The savages who attack us don't get exhausted, they even thrive on their sadism and bestiality.

If that weren't the case, if the lord and his cronies didn't hold that view, the white armored vehicles (they are already making our ears hurt here in Sarajevo) would have been posted at some point between Ilidža and Hadžići a long time ago, and things would look somewhat different. The secret behind this spring's fallen cherries, ruined potatoes, and unpicked strawberries is not what we've been told.

That is why the parcel that came today is not meant for our survival. It is here to force us to our knees, to do their bidding. Luckily, we don't get our energy from their protein, but from very different sources. We'll return to that later.

7 August 1992

SHELL WITH A "DEDICATION"

Planes appeared over Sarajevo, and helicopters over the surrounding countryside. When this happened, the entire staff of *Oslobodenje* hit the floor. Everyone, of course, has his or her own theory about supporting walls and partitions; everyone knows which wall is safe, and which spot between large windows is not. But each time a new shell arrives, it also destroys (besides a few walls and partitions) these amateur safety theories. Explosive shells, tank missiles that do not explode, rockets from portable launchers—no one knows which are the worst.

It's amazing the way people talk about these things, yelling from around corners and under tables. Less than a month ago I saw with my own eyes women fainting as they heard shells whistle overhead. Now, calmly, one might even say analytically, they determine the range, type, and caliber, and debate where it will land, and what kind of destruction it will cause.

Another horrible explosion, smoke, windows shattering, wood cracking. My office, my third since the beginning of the war, has disappeared. . . .

Now in its place is a pile of brick, glass, metal, and some torn posters I had dragged around the world with me for the last fifteen years. Out of a mound of rubble that still seems to be hissing I pull the tail of the shell whose body has wreaked this havoc. It is a small object, olive green, still hot, with ten ailerons and the inscription: KB 1986—82 mm. It was launched from an emplacement in Nedžarići that has been known as the House of Santa Claus since the day gunners from there fired on a busload of children trying to leave the city.

After that, at least fifteen more rounds of the same type, but even more powerful, 120 mm, struck the big charred concrete skeleton of *Oslobodenje*—where we've been producing the newspaper in the basement.

Yet life goes on. Within an absolute communications blockade, exchange takes place through the most unbelievable filaments, and people from all corners of the world connect with news, messages, a few parcels, or simply a word to let others know they're alive and well. Radio amateurs are doing a heroic job, achieving the impossible. I overheard a few words spoken from the heart and soul after a hundred hours of silence, transmitted to a distant ear: "What did she say to me now?" "She said the children have grown." "What?" "That they've grown." "What is she saying now?" "That she loves you." "Excuse me?" "She says she loves you, can you hear me?" "I can't hear you." "That's all right, she's doing well."

Then comes yet another little olive-green KB 1986—82 mm. How long, for God's sake? Izetbegović has written yet another gentle letter to someone out there.

IMITATION OF LIFE

Our story, I'm afraid, is totally unreal. Sometimes I tell myself that people outside who don't know what is happening here must think that we're insane. All they need to do to get that impression from a distance, is follow the people and events of Sarajevo for a little while. We, obviously, don't see it like this, but that's because we're lost in our daily troubles, and maybe also because we have so little energy left in the batteries that keep life running.

On Saturday, for instance, an elderly woman knocked on my door holding a note pad in her hand, explaining that she was collecting money for electricity. However, as I soon learned, it wasn't really a question of paying electricity bills, but only of collecting money. After exchanging only a few words it became clear to me what she was after. She said, politely and without the least embarrassment, "If you could pay for April, May, and June, that would be three thousand dinars." Now, three thousand dinars is nothing—it's six kilograms of bread, when you can get it—but it is a considerable sum for those who are destitute.

Thank God, now my friends are sharing the place with me and we have some means, since we sell our damned little newspaper, almost raising enough to cover our salaries. So we gave the woman fifteen thousand dinars, and

SARAJEVO

she told us that would be enough for three more families
who have nothing. She left satisfied.

Something similar happened on a bus that appeared out
of nowhere, on a nonscheduled run along the city's main
thoroughfare. The driver announced to us that he was
going up to the television building and back. Right in front
of us, a woman asked the conductor (who sat in his seat, in
accordance with the regulations) how much the fare was.
"If you have money, it's three dinars. If you don't, pay us
when the war is over," the charming conductor told her.

We offered to pay the (as it turned out) penniless
woman's fare, but the conductor wouldn't hear of it.
"Please, it's out of the question. Our company, the municipal transportation enterprise, offers free rides to fellow
citizens who have to get to work." Way to go! We had a nice
ride, feeling less afraid than usual. Such a bus had to be
immune to mortar shells and sniper bullets. Hopes of that
sort are all we have left. Everything else is only ersatz
existence.

Yesterday afternoon six of us were sitting in a makeshift
café, having a quick wartime drink, and discussing some
work we had to finish by today, so we agreed that we would
meet today at the same time in the same place. But our date
was cancelled because two of the six are now hospitalized.
Zdravko had to have shrapnel removed from a leg and an
arm, and the doctors are still struggling to save Goran's leg,
perhaps even his life. My other friend Goran and I happened to pass the spot where the shell exploded and where,
only moments before, Zdravko Petrović and Goran Stapić
had been wounded. Our lives have been reduced to the
simple matter of getting hit or not getting hit; that's all.

Yesterday Goran and I moved into a new office, the third

we've had since the beginning of the war, only to find it full of shrapnel and broken glass this morning. After we cleaned up and put everything back on its feet again, we realized that nothing worked, for another reason entirely. There was no electricity—the phones and fax machine were dead, and no radio or television.

The only thing that worked this morning was the neighborhood sniper, busy as ever. I would like to know how much they're paying him for all the overtime he's putting in. In fact, how *do* they deal with the matter of pay? I'm told that foreigners have taken all their hard currency, and their ridiculous Serbian dinars are worthless everywhere, even in Ilidža. It truly is an imitation of life, but it's better than nothing.

THE DETAINEES OF SARAJEVO

I see the world is somewhat flustered by its discovery of concentration camps in Bosnia-Herzegovina. They really seem pretty worked up over "indications" that the stories they've heard about these camps may turn out to be true. . . .

Given that the West is a so-called empirical society, it needs to confirm the latest news, black on white, or even better, red on white, before such "indications" can be accepted as referring to anything tangible. In any case, there is a great deal of excitement and agitation, and there is no end to a new wave of stories about the need for an intervention of some kind to clean the camps of their "malnourished political detainees, sentenced according to regular procedures," as the prisoners are referred to so eloquently by our regional Himmler, Radovan Karadžić.

The gentlemen of CNN, longing for another Desert Storm, suddenly began turning up the heat in support of a military intervention, whose outcome could be a latter-day General Patton's entry into the camps as a liberator, bearing the flag of American freedom. It looks as if things are getting serious.

Two nights in a row, while we still had electricity, we watched an hour-long American television program devoted to us. A whole hour is not to be sneezed at, considering that every second of CNN's summer programming costs millions of dollars. In other words, they sniffed out new business, and we want to thank them for it. The critical mass of deaths here may finally be sufficient to make something happen. As for the critical mass of suffering, it is already so high that any action, were it to come, would be too late for us to forgive everyone for what has occurred already. First of all, how could we forgive their reluctance to see or recognize the existence of concentration camps when they have been there to be seen by squirrels on every bough?

The story of the camps began, unfolded, and is drawing to an end right here, in Sarajevo, the biggest concentration camp the world has ever seen, and it is unlikely the world will ever witness one of its size again.

In the concentration camps we know from history, people were held prisoner without any opportunity to move from place to place. That's how it is here. Every now and then those people were given a few spoonfuls of food, just like here. They were deprived of all the rights fixed and enumerated in international declarations and codes, just like here. Collaborators and traitors, the Fifth Column, had a chance to survive. Like here. The inmates had no way of communicating with their relatives and friends on the outside taken away from them. From time to time they might have succeeded in getting a torn-up parcel with a censored letter. Here too. And finally, inmates from those camps were murdered according to some criminal "rationale": the old, the weak, the Jews, the Communists, the gypsies, those accused of anything at all.

Here no such rationale applies. We are being murdered

at random, without rationale. True, we are all guilty of not being *chetniks*; guilty of not being able to convince the world that our only wish is to live according to the way those fat declarations say how life can, and has the right to, be lived. Or is it simply that the way we want to live interferes with the great plans of those who fashion the destiny of the world?

Actually, it is their opinion that we have chosen a bad time and place to exist at all. True, the moment may be inopportune. As for the place, we like it, and we have no intention to look for another—even though it has become, whether or not you choose to recognize it, a concentration camp in the strict sense of the term.

12 August 1992

SARAJEVANS BLIND A SNIPER

It isn't easy to decide who wages the more dangerous and bloody war in the streets of Sarajevo: those who try their damnedest to turn this city into a distant memory, or those who oppose the annihilation with all their might, who refuse to die or disappear. Yesterday, between one streetcar stop (at the big downtown department store) and the next (Marindvor), six people were killed and twenty wounded. Although there has been no official announcement, we also know that two mortar shells killed five children and wounded at least twenty. We don't even know if that's the extent of it; probably not. People are shot and killed every day, day after day, and the casualty lists are never up to date.

One of the faces of Sarajevo is that of a city in which one lives, works, and dies as if in a cell; a whole city bent on survival at any cost. The other face of Sarajevo is so incredible, in its own way, that it is hard to describe to anyone who isn't here. The will to live, a strength gathered every morning from God-knows-where that makes it possible to reconstruct, every day, what was destroyed and ravaged the day before. An unrivaled sensitivity in mending these lifelines that seem unmendable: hope, perseverance, and faith.

Everything, but everything, here has changed, and nothing is how it used to be. You no longer walk the same streets you did before, you go new ways, decided upon only by the imperatives of survival. You no longer sit where you used to sit, nor sleep where you used to sleep.

On what used to be called Kulovićeva Street (I can't remember its new name), right next to the Hotel Belgrade (our crowd now calls it Hotel Sarajevo), a banner has appeared just like that, spontaneously, the biggest one I've ever seen. From the top of a relatively tall building, attached to it by ropes, this banner goes all the way down to the sidewalk. Thanks to this huge curtain that now flutters gently in the summer breeze, the killers in the hills can no longer see pedestrians on the main thoroughfare. That's how the city's worst snipers have been blinded. Our gang delights in the thought of a *chetnik* getting bent out of shape. "Just imagine how pissed off he must have been when he found out this morning that he can't see anything," comments with great satisfaction an elderly gentleman as he stands behind a building and admires the superb banner.

Life finds all sorts of ways to animate the city. Today everybody is talking about the "Sugar House crossroads" at Bašćaršija, where you can get drinking water again, of dubious quality but nevertheless drinkable. At Ramiz's there is even ice cream, five flavors, suddenly present like a mirage. We think it the best ice cream in the world, the envy of the Italians. Yesterday Alen moved his store into the former "Sport" next to "Egypt," Sarajevo's best pastry shop, and in his store you can find soap, toilet paper, according to some, even bouillon cubes for soups and sauces, slacks for one hundred and fifty thousand dinars, light bulbs for four thousand. The enterprising fellow from

Ilidža has even managed to procure some toothpaste from God-knows-where. Outside, at a corner of the market, tourist maps of Sarajevo are selling like halva. Some are old and creased, but it is wonderful to see them.

The new topology of the city has been a pain in the neck to all of us, with its hundreds of alleys and crossroads and quarters we had never heard of until now. Now we talk about them all the time—either because of crimes that have been committed there, or because of the audacious and formidable street gangs of young kids that make life hard for the people in those places.

More mortar shells rain down on the city. People at the TV station call to tell me that some boys from Zagreb have managed to enter the city, and that they have a parcel for me.

I've been told that small sandwiches with *kajmak* cheese* are available at a refreshment stand next to the College of Economics—incredible! I have to see this, take notes, take photographs. A day will come when they won't believe us. Just like yesterday, I couldn't believe my eyes when a friend, an ambassador, appeared on my doorstep, brought in by a Hercules transport plane; he came to Sarajevo because he's part of our crowd.

Here life and death are locked in ferocious combat, forever trying to gain the upper hand. At the moment one can't say which of the two stands the better chance of winning.

*A kind of cream cheese.

THE LITTLE POWERMONGERS

The number of people you can get in touch with in this city shrinks every day. There are no cars: they're either wrecked, stolen, confiscated, or out of gas. The shelling and the snipers have made walking more dangerous than any hand-to-hand combat on the front lines. So driving and walking are out. And now they've started taking people's phones away. I don't know of anyone to whom this has happened who doesn't think life might become impossible here if conditions continue to be dictated by the heroes of our war offices.

Briefly: Someone has come to the conclusion that a Fifth Column is making use of the phone lines to inform the *chetniks* how to correct their aim, where to shoot and whom to hit. Very conscientiously, local patriotic defense teams have mounted an implacable assault on Sarajevo's telephones. In an unparalleled demonstration of patriotism and officious zeal left over from the old days of the secret police, they have cut off the few phones that were genuine lifelines for entire streets and districts. Naturally, abandoned telephones found in some apartments have been put under strict surveillance by faithful members of the local "revolutionary guard." This will make it impossible for anyone to collaborate with the enemy. Or so they believe.

This mania has spread with pestilential rapidity from

the quarters nearest the *chetnik* lines to every other part of the city, imprisoned, encircled, and isolated as it is. Those of us who are left—still without water, electricity, radio, television, and now without the telephone—are nothing but sacrificial beasts, deprived of all rights except the right to loneliness, hunger, humiliation, and death.

In popular quarters, in dark basements, on the landings of apartment buildings these new *Kapos** are gathering to make decisions on the local level (against which there is no recourse) as to who gets to keep his phone and who has it cut off until some other decision has been reached.

But to what extent does the telephone really serve the *chetniks* as a "means of transmission," when every little kid knows that signals of this type can be transmitted in a thousand different ways: from a pair of underpants on a line to curtains either open or shut. Not to mention the thousands of walkie-talkies in town, or even more sophisticated methods, such as whispering. A more serious side to this story is posed by the fact that every little functionary is now convinced that he has the power to decide who has the right to use the telephone, who is potentially one of "ours," who potentially "theirs."

Never for one second was I as afraid of shells exploding below my window as I am of certain professional patriots, whose number has grown enormously during the hundred and fifty days of this war. Imagine how many of them there will be at the end of the madness! In these days of war, I have begun to fear peace and the people who may one day turn this local patriotic lobby into a real state. Not to mention that it was some among them who got us into this mess in the first place.

---

*Inmates of Nazi concentration camps charged by the S.S. with supervising powers over prisoners.

18 August 1992

THE JEWS LEAVE,
SARAJEVO DISAPPEARS

There are days when even the most stubborn optimists feel the pinch, when you just feel like saying the hell with everything, packing a small bag, and sneaking away under cover of darkness, to who-cares-which side, toward that disgusting line that surrounds the city like a band of steel and transforms us into plain, little, illegitimate, insignificant creatures. That's how things have been yesterday and today. Good feelings have faded among those who were so excited over the news from New York. Too bad.

Again there is no electricity, no water, and wild snipers are aiming at workers who have come to repair the broken cables. Next to the electrical power station, at the fountain, a woman was killed while she tried to fill her bucket. In the parks people lop green branches by the hundreds off the trees. Looking out my window, I saw a man, well groomed and wearing a neatly ironed white shirt, bend down to pick up a cigarette butt that had lain there God knows how long. I can imagine what he must have felt like as our eyes met; for a moment, his hand hovered over the butt before he picked it up.

Everybody is talking about next winter, that it is approaching, slowly but steadily. Despair envelops the city since, apparently, there is no way out of this madness. At the hospital, a thirteen-year-old girl who had lost her right arm and left hand tried to commit suicide. She didn't succeed—not this time.

We are printing the final issues of our newspaper since permission hasn't been granted to have newsprint delivered to the city, and we are unable to leave. Permission to leave isn't granted by "ours," nor by "theirs," nor by UNPROFOR, nor by the High Commission on Refugees.

Dolled-up delegations from a happy, distant world come to Sarajevo on day trips, only to verify prison conditions and see whether or not there is any difference between how imprisoned *chetniks* are treated here compared to those in places like Omarska and Manjača, where the unfortunate internees never had the chance to choose their first or last names at birth.

Then the emissaries pat us on the back and congratulate us, having satisfied themselves that *chetniks* are doing just fine in our prisons. We are truly a civilized people, so we deserve a little more macaroni and rice, and maybe even a few bottles of vitamins for kids four months old and up.

So it goes in Sarajevo, today as yesterday; tomorrow will be even worse. If there still is a Sarajevo, which is hard to say after the departure of its Jews, who have already packed their bags. The last seven hundred are about to go, members of a community that was one of the largest in this part of the world, people who were the marrow and fabric of Sarajevo, along with the Muslims, Croats, and Serbs. I remember being told, one night in Jerusalem, that Sarajevo was the only city in the world, after Jerusalem, where members of the three great world religions lived in harmony. Now the Jews of Sarajevo have to leave for a safe haven if they want to survive. Their most precious site, their old cemetery, a site of tremendous symbolic and historic value, has become a major stronghold of the *chetniks* of Sarajevo. It has been dug up, leveled, and paved. It has become an accursed place because of the snipers that terrorize the city.

Remembering how sincerely the Muslims had saved the lives of these Jews fifty years ago, the Jews today do not want to leave by themselves; they want to bring their friends and neighbors into temporary exile, but the "international humanitarians" will not let them. "Who will stay, if everybody leaves?" they asked. Translated into the language of the actual events taking place here, with a touch of sarcasm, one could also put it like this: "Why don't you all just die, it makes no sense for some to be saved while others have to stay." Only today do I realize how right Zdravko Grebo was when, during the presidential campaign a year ago, he launched the slogan "We'll all die together."

The Jews will return one day, I'm sure of that. In the meantime, their departure marks the beginning of the execution of the Karadžić Plan. If people who have lived in Sarajevo for five centuries leave the city, this will no longer be the same Sarajevo. Five hundred years, that's how long it's been since Sephardic Jews came to these parts, and now they have to leave in order to survive. The circle is closing. The plan relayed from one monster to another, Ćosić to Karadžić, is being carried out: "Keep doing what you're doing, until what once seemed impossible becomes possible."

1 October 1992

TO OBLITERATE WHAT HAS
ALREADY BEEN DESTROYED

Sarajevo has spent another long—too long—night at rest with its eyes open, waiting for a light that never came after a day and night of darkness. Another cold gray morning, and we all silently worked the switches, turning the heaters on and off, hoping for something to happen, but they stayed cold as we settled down to wait for another night.

Some of us, carrying buckets, stand in line for water. There is practically only one fountain left, which provides a meager trickle. Others go and collect branches in what's left of the parks and the woods. Still others hide in their apartments, whose windows have been "repaired" with sheets or cardboard, as they struggle with their own thoughts. "Till when, why, in the name of what?"

This morning the main dispatcher from the electric company announced on the radio that there was no juice in Sarajevo and that one had better not even expect it today. He said the technicians were doing the best they could, but the *chetniks* kept destroying as well as they could too. Colonel Sartre, the French commandant of an UNPROFOR battalion charged with logistical support, told me with a touch of resignation, "Everything you fix, they manage to break again. It's like the labors of Sisyphus, but there's nothing we can do about it. We'll make whatever repairs we can."

No question, the man was honestly deflated. Unfortunately, no one talks about resignation anymore. Our problem no longer has anything to do with psychological states; it is now a matter of survival. There is no more food. I know dozens of people who count themselves lucky if they manage to find a slice of bread and half a glass of tea in which to dip it. *Every other day*. I know others who don't even get that much. The last kilos of flour have been used up, even though the kitchen stove doesn't work. All reserves and hope, however feeble, have fled with the smoke from our improvised ovens in the streets.

In spite of everything, Sarajevo goes on breathing, warming its frozen feet by jumping in place, whimpering but still alive. Radio and television keep on broadcasting, thanks to the last drops of diesel fuel in their generators. We keep up with what goes on around us. We hear messages sent to us by people with full bellies, but we also know how many have died in, and for, the rest of Bosnia-Herzegovina.

There are fewer and fewer streets in this city. Fewer and fewer buildings, and, unfortunately, fewer and fewer people. Those up in the hills haven't grown weary; they are now shooting at what was destroyed a long time ago. Right now, this very second, their tanks are firing at the charred stump of the *Oslobodenje* building again. That former beauty is now just a heap of misery, memories, and concrete.

How much ammunition do they have in reserve to keep up this kind of thing? And we must be feeling pretty miserable, not even to look for a place to be safe while the shooting goes on. We don't even look at each other anymore as the walls shake. What would be the point? We're here, and here we'll stay until it's over. We no longer sing as we used to a month or two ago. We probably laugh less and are silent longer, because everything has already been said. But we're still here.

I also notice that, on the radio, we hear fewer enthusiastic announcements of counterattacks designed to break the blockade of Sarajevo; less of that happy warrior talk. Or does it just seem that way? It does seem to me that our boys are making more progress than when there was more singing and less shooting. Dedication is now taken for granted, so verbal declarations are no longer necessary. Everybody asks himself what direction Sarajevo will take once the siege is broken. Toward what universe will it go? Into the desert of this divided and desolate world?

Sarajevo, this unique city, has no shelter but itself, even as we find ourselves famished and frozen in it. What does it matter that a kilo of potatoes already costs fifteen or twenty German marks, meat and cabbage twice as much, when you can't find any of them anyway. There is nothing to be had, but we'll get by. I ask myself what it would be like if these things were available, but no one knew how to distribute them fairly.

2 October 1992

HUNGER AND PIGEONS

Electricity is slowly returning to some parts of town, and so is running water; here and there even a telephone or two. But there is no bread, and people are again getting killed by shells exploding in the streets, exploding any hope of one day seeing this horror come to an end.

Blue Helmets arrive, saying they need three weeks to position themselves on certain roads, after which they will proceed "according to our plan." If it takes them another three weeks to do that, let's see how far they get. I don't know if there will be anyone left to meet them in Sarajevo, at Gradačac, or at Jajce, when they come marching in. The question, of course, arises as to whether or not they really want to find anyone there.

But when I watch what is going on around me, and when I listen to the new sweetheart of the Srna news agency, Magnusson, acting as a spokesman for the UNPROFOR, I have my doubts. That spokesman was really shaken up when soldiers of the Bosnian Army used a huge container, probably filled with explosives, to block the road between the airport and the city, in order to "cut the axis along which foodstuffs are transported to the city from the airport."

It is true that the Bosnian Army did that. It is also true

that trucks loaded with food could no longer reach the city. And it is true that Mr. Magnusson flew into a rage when he saw this, and that many people abroad were glad to be enraged, at long last. Mr. Magnusson then transformed his rage into the first threat ever uttered by an official representative of the Protection Force, saying that "the Blue Helmets will open fire." Regrettably, the threat was directed at Bosnia-Herzegovina's legitimate forces. And obviously Mr. Magnusson left out the essentials.

Abroad, the notorious container was represented as an obstacle erected between good humanitarians and bad Bosnian soldiers. But the real reason it was planted in the middle of that road was that numerous *chetnik* tanks had entered the airport area, which is (supposedly) under the control of Magnusson's soldiers. And those tanks were preparing to break through the Bosnian defenses they had been attacking for days, in order to enter the city.

How come *chetnik* tanks were at the airport, when UN documents state that it has been a demilitarized zone for many days? Why doesn't Mr. Magnusson accept an alternative route to the city for his convoys? Through Donja, for instance, which is out of range for the *chetnik* tanks? Why hasn't Mr. Magnusson threatened to open fire on the *chetniks*? It is they who have for days on end prevented workers from repairing our electric and gas lines. Why does he get so upset when we erect barricades against *chetnik* tanks stationed at "his" airport? Oh, Magnusson, Magnusson . . .

Whatever his reasons, some good has come of this. Without the container episode, we never would have known that the Protection Force has the right to open fire. Every time the *chetniks* shot at them, chased them off, destroyed one of their vehicles, or played some other dirty trick on them, we kept thinking: Poor guys, what can they do, when they're not allowed to return fire? It's not in their mandate, as they say, like true professionals. But now that same mandate allows them to fire on the shield put up against the *chetnik* tanks, and on those who have erected that obstacle!

That is all I have to say on the question of shooting. Everything else is the same. In the dark of night, people jostle each other in the street trying to catch rainwater in their buckets. For several days, snails were the fashion. Our chefs demonstrated that they can be prepared in several different ways. But now there are no more snails. Maybe it got too cold; maybe they've all been eaten.

The most resourceful among us have taken to hunting and trapping pigeons. Unfortunately, the kids won't touch the bird once it's on their plate. Some street kids have even formed gangs to fight those who catch pigeons. Strange children, these, who would rather die of hunger than stay alive if it means eating a dead pigeon. Good Lord, what chance of survival does Sarajevo have with such children? The others up in the hills resolved that dilemma a long time ago. For them it is not a question of pigeons. And therein lies the difference between us.

LEARNING BY WOUNDS
AND LIES

A lot less of Sarajevo and a lot more grief and sorrow than there was a month ago. Since then, life has become a spasm of survival, a battle for the vital minimum, scurrying around looking for what can be cut, sawn off, or scavenged from what is left of buildings, to make it through another day. People have stopped thinking about shells, snipers, and shrapnel; that's all just taken for granted.

Despair grows more intense with the approach of winter, already on our doorstep. The sleety rainwater that filled our bathtubs and pots also gave us the first breath of white death. Shot-out windows, broken-down doors, holes in the walls look like harbingers of a white inferno that will not be easy to get through.

Some quarters are already frosty, since there is no electricity, no running water, no gas. Hospitals have no more beds for the sick and wounded. Blood transfusions can be given only to those whose relatives have managed to pull strings, but that won't work with drugs and antibiotics. Yet I have seen large stores of them in various warehouses on the outskirts, though aid destined for the city never seems to get here.

Sarajevans no longer trust anyone. How could they? For

the last month, only the most fortunate have managed to get access to a kilo of flour and a half liter of cooking oil. Luckily, since we don't have batteries, we don't even get news about the humanitarian corridors and convoys. But we know that Bosanski Brod has fallen; that it is no longer possible to leave our ill-fated state, not by any road; that an UNPROFOR officer stated in a report that he was "disappointed" by the behavior of a *chetnik* who had chased him away from an area where people were working on the restoration of water supplies to the city. We truly feel for this man's disappointment.

There are thousands of other things that we don't know, and we're better off not knowing. People can't imagine what lies are being told about them in the foreign press. What lies are being told about what is happening here. With what impertinence lies are being used to sow discord among the few who have stayed in Sarajevo. It's true that all our grief and worry have shattered our nerves; true that we have less strength to smile, or to be generous in any way. But what we still have of Sarajevo is on its feet, and resisting. Things look different here from what some on the outside are hoping.

If only we could have a couple of days of electricity, and water for two hours a day to refill our buckets of drinking water, the rest would come from heaven and the city would be transformed. And the next cutoff would be met differently. People have learned many things these past twenty days. They have learned how to be grateful for a bit of rain, how to wash their hair with cold water, how to cook from whatever they have a food made with flour that is like bread, but isn't, and how to spread on it things that were never meant to be spread.

Sarajevo learns from its wounds as well as from the lies and deceptions of the world outside; in some strange ways, the city feels all the good things intended for it in its gut, even though they never arrive here. Life is filled with variety, I guess, and you can never really learn about it all. Those on the outside will know less and less about what life is really like.

MINISTERS OF DISTANT AFFAIRS

In Sarajevo, politics have become more important than ordinary life, and that is bad. As if to be a Muslim, a Croat, or a Serb were more important than everyone surviving the winter; as if the ministers (whether competent or not) were more important than water and electricity; the cantonization plans and Geneva more important than diseases and wounds. Yet this abundance of politics, this parody of politics, is less important than a child's cold, not to mention everything else happening here.

After a light-year's absence, the venerable Mr. Silajdžić, Minister of Distant, not Present, Affairs, arrived in Sarajevo. He gave a press conference that turned into a celebration of his personal accomplishments, and an attack on the press, after which he left. Nine out of ten of our other ministers have done less than that, but they too have left. One can count on the fingers of one hand those among them who are abroad but continue working for the people who stayed. A question arises: Why should we take an interest in politics when it was politics that led us into this disaster, and when our rare moments of happiness—or at least our ordinary, normal moments—can only be found in the details of our daily lives, such as they are?

It's a little nicer in town than a week or two ago. The so-called humanitarian aid got here yesterday. The lines in front of the distribution offices are endless, but people who have been perennially searching for food say that the aid is "super, it's never been better." "Super" means two cans of pâté per person, a few plastic bags with three centiliters (just about the size of a shot of brandy) of olive oil, five hundred grams of flour, two hundred grams of cheese, and—hang on to your hats—five hundred grams of potatoes. At the market potatoes cost twenty marks a kilo, just like onions, but ten marks less than a liter of oil. You can also get a can of tomatoes per family ration card—in other words, for a whole "refuge apartment"—so that if you'd like to follow the Herzegovinian recipe for plain boiled rice, you can make it a little red.

Speaking of the market, there are a few other little improvements. Coal has arrived, at fifty marks a sack. A liter of fuel for lamps, to which you can add some salt, so it'll burn longer, goes for ten marks. A pack of cigarettes, three marks. For those who prefer to price things in our currency, here are a few more prices: a pack of chewing gum, six hundred dinars; a bag of candy, one thousand dinars; a bottle of draft beer, two thousand dinars. The average pensioner here pulls in ten thousand dinars a month, so you can figure it out for yourself.

Of course, you can go for straight bartering, like in the times we seem to have again become part of. A liter of lamp fuel is worth three kilos of sugar, a can of anything gets you ten kilos of flour. Or, as someone said recently, ten Rembrandts for two liters of cooking oil. Here we know the true value of things.

It's much nicer to talk of subjects like this with the remaining Sarajevans you bump into on the street than it is to talk about politics. In fact, these casual street conversations are the nicest part of our lives. All of us who are here, who stayed, have gotten to know each other quite well, one way or another. And nobody has anything new to say to anyone, about how they are, where they've been, and what they're doing. Such things are not even discussed. We all know that we're out looking for bread or collecting rainwater, that we're trying to insulate our windows with whatever we happen to come upon, that we're dragging home branches of trees from the parks.

Our degree of humanism or culture is shown only by the type of branch we pick: a dead one, or one that is still green. In other words, do you just bend down and collect what's on the ground already, broken and abandoned, or do you break off and cut some living branches to take with you?

Because of all this, one talks of other things marching down the street. Of magnificent pedigree dogs abandoned by their owners because they can no longer feed them, of such masters and their morals. One also talks about whether we'll ever reforest the surroundings, or whether anyone has any thoughts on what to do, when the time comes, with all the crushed concrete, gravel, broken glass from the destroyed buildings, office towers, and hovels; or why the postal authorities lied to us when they said there wouldn't be any telephone service for three years—even though now they're asking us for eight to ten marks to reconnect the old lines?

All in all, this everyday life is much more pleasant than politics. Maybe because we feel so cut off from politics; not that this wasn't our own choice, but that's just how it is.

VIDEO LETTERS FROM PARIS

Yesterday we watched an interesting show on TV. Of course, by "we" I mean those who had electricity. The dispatches say that sixty percent of the still-standing buildings can be reconnected to the distribution network; God knows what the percentage really is. No matter, this really has little to do with the show I'm talking about, though it may have everything to do with it, depending on how you see it. . . . The broadcast consisted of video letters exchanged between Paris and Sarajevo. Over there, in the City of Light, they even titled theirs "Homage to Sarajevo," but the people here left theirs untitled, they simply shot a film and sent it to Paris.

So, first a bunch of intellectuals there sat around a table and talked of how to help our culture vultures, in a cultural way. The discussion was actually moving and sincere. Costa Gavras said that he would like his new film to premiere in Sarajevo. Others said it would be nice if our ravaged city could become the official headquarters of certain renowned European cultural institutions. This would show the rest of the world that the struggle in Sarajevo is a fight for multiculturalism and religious coexistence, the first prerequisites for "cultural exchange" and the "humanization of humankind."

All the people around the table were drinking tea in pretty china cups poured from an even prettier rustic teapot. All kidding aside, the whole thing *was* well put together, and it showed genuine feeling and understanding. The discussion was recorded three months ago, on the thirty-first of July, but we hadn't been able to see it until now.

Last night, the big names of Sarajevo's cultural and intellectual circles graciously responded to the offer made by their Parisian colleagues. There was no tea, no china, not even a table or any lights. They sat in our burned-out City Hall, in the charred library that once preserved our whole past, as well as a good part of our future.

Sidran talked about the "measure of evil," different today from three months ago. Ljubović told the story of his "Bosnian rooms." The furniture that once was in those rooms is now being sold at a flea market in Belgrade. The salesmen are people who "visited" these rooms in Grbavica, where Ljubović managed to escape from them "in sneakers and no socks," which he had no time to find. Others told similar stories: Ibrišimović, Bibanović, Kalcina, Kenović. . . .

At the end, Marko Vešović addressed a few words to our Parisian friends from where he sat, in a broken van before the demolished TV building, speaking in a cracked voice. He thanked Costa Gavras for the generous gesture to premiere his movie in Sarajevo, for which there definitely would be an audience, but pointed out that he would also have to send along a movie theater in which to show it. He said that it was good to think in such a cultured way about cultural matters over here, but that even just *thinking* here was difficult now—not to mention thinking about culture—when *chetnik* dynamite is blowing Muslim and Croat places of worship sky-high. "How can we think about culture when at Ahmatovići, only kilometers from Sarajevo, the *chetniks* ushered fifty people into a bus and then blew it to bits?" I'm sure Marko had more to say, but it was difficult for him to continue, surrounded as he was by all the devastation, with smoke pouring from the windows of rooms in which everything that had been written or recorded in this region for centuries was stored. After that we didn't watch anything. The power was cut off. I'm told that our video response is on its way to Paris.

We felt a little uneasy. Maybe we didn't respond in quite the friendly way with which we were approached. Maybe it all could have been handled with more aplomb, perhaps we could have been more appreciative. Maybe Ljubović's socks weren't all that important, or Avdo's statement on "the progress of evil" could have been more nuanced. But who knows, maybe it was right the way it was.

THE MADNESS, THE NAUSEA

By the look of it, it is a normal November day. The sun is shining. Since this morning, "nothing" but some sniper fire and bursts from antiaircraft guns directed at crossroads exposed to view from the slopes of Trebević.

"I never noticed how high that hill was, and that it's practically in town," a friend said to me recently while grabbing my hand to hurry me across a street with a view of Trebević. More and more of us don't feel like running across such streets anymore. We're fed up with running, hiding, bending, taking cover. A ten-year-old boy was killed yesterday while sitting at a table in his room. No warning whatsoever.

Trebević keeps growing taller and taller as leaves keep falling and trees keep getting cut down. You can't escape from that hill, you can't push it away or turn your back on it. How we once loved it, pampered and protected it—even from ourselves. This just shows that they have achieved one of their monstrous goals: involuntarily, silently, we have become divided. Us and Trebević; us and Pale; us and Romanija, Banja Luka, Jahorina . . .

Last night we watched a truly unbelievable commercial they produced for Srna TV. They've collected the most enticing pictures from all over the world; you know, happy kids, their faces smeared with chocolate, platefuls of lobster (as if they had grown up on it!), beautiful beaches and seascapes, to say finally, more or less in so many words: "If, instead of war, suffering, penury, and misery, instead of famine and destruction you want all this again—*choose partition!*" It's hard to comprehend so much xenophobia, such a need to be only among your own (with a plateful of lobster, to be sure), such an inability to adapt to any other way of life. Nevertheless, they've succeeded. Madness seems to be contagious, while the normal, humane, intelligent, and rational just doesn't pass muster.

They've dragged us down with them, so now we hate Trebević and Pale. Our nostalgia for Jahorina has changed into resignation, and any notion of a journey East brings on a feeling of nausea. They are no doubt pleased that this is so. I am not. We never wanted to have more than they had, but that wasn't enough for them.

A man whom we had great respect for, despite the fact that he was one of the harshest critics of the press, has finally and definitely left the city: Stjepan Kljujić, Croat citizen of Sarajevo. He held his post by the will of the people, as an elected official. Now he has left by order of "the representatives of the people," without a vote. My friend and colleague Gojko Borić had this to say in *Oslobodenje*:

> When democratic procedure is replaced by decrees from political parties, one wonders if that really is the form of government which the people expressed their confidence in two years ago, after hearing its promises of democracy. The problem lies not in admitting that Bosnia-Herzegovina won't be a democratic country for many years to come, but in admitting that it will be an antidemocratic one. That is the

political, legal, and ethical context in which the "Kljujić case" has to be seen. The reshuffle in question has taken place in the darkness of anarchy and bloody national division. When the light returns, we shall see its true meaning and purpose.

With Gojko's permission, I would like to add one more sentence: "If the light ever does return."

Since nothing good seems to come of politics and grand statements, there's nothing left for us but to return to our everyday existence, such as it is. On that front, here is some news: There no longer is a zoo in the Valley of the Pioneers. The last grizzly bear has died—quietly, they say. He out-lived all the lions, and tigers, and wolves, and even the foxes; they proved less resistant to starvation than he did. We also hear that a few ponies are still wandering around in that no-man's-land, which the hill people have barred to the guardians of childhood delight—the zoo keepers can't enter because of the *chetniks*. Those ponies are the last survivors; all the others have been caught and butchered. Someone claims to have seen a peacock and a white swan, both solitary, roaming in sad freedom.

19 November 1992

SONGS IN DOBRINJA

When the war started in Sarajevo, more than a few people brought up Dobrinja to evoke the worst a war can bring: hunger, death, total isolation, abandonment and injustice, tanks below your window, deportations, cigarettes made of tea used ten times over, a handful of rice to last ten days, three rifles to defend a thousand people, and continuous fear of what the next hour would bring. . . . What those people said then about Dobrinja was true. Nevertheless, it is also true that it is people who matter, not the war; what remains important is the will, the faith, the inner strength undreamed of in peacetime, all those things that can give birth to defiance, perseverance, solidarity, and knowledge.

In Sarajevo, Dobrinja is now spoken of a lot, with good reason. What has happened there is a miracle of the kind only human beings, in the noble sense of the term, are able to perform. More and more frequently you hear voices singing in this suburb, encircled and almost completely surrounded by war-torn zones dominated by snipers and heavy machine guns. Fewer and fewer inhabitants of Dobrinja are willing to "go to the city," and once here, they want to return to Dobrinja. There, apparently, it is not the war but humanity that has gained the upper hand. Whatever the ultimate outcome, in Dobrinja Sarajevo has won its greatest battle. Actually, it would be more honest to come right out and say it: Dobrinja justifies all those secret hopes that while Sarajevo might be destroyed, it will never be vanquished.

From the trauma brought on by days and nights of isolation and hiding from the bloodsuckers lurking at every doorstep, a resistance movement was born—precise in its actions and organization. And now it has become a kind of "commune" with no equal in the region. That part of the city leads its own life, a life envied by all the "normal" people in the rest of the city, even if they won't say so openly. In Dobrinja, people know who is who. They know how many people live there, what shape their apartments are in, who can share and who can't, who is able to bear arms, who can wash and clean, cook, or help out—and who can write, sing, or act. Today Dobrinja knows all the old people within its borders who are homebound and need to get whatever they have coming to them right at the door. Dobrinja also knows of all its children who have been left without mothers or fathers, children for whom this little city tries, insofar as it is possible, to compensate for their irredeemable loss.

The Blue Helmets stationed at the neighboring airport happily go to Dobrinja, not returning to their barracks as soon as they've distributed their aid packages, but lingering in people's apartments, in the improvised clubs and sand-bagged meeting places where people hang out and talk. A few days ago the Helmets sang a French song dedicated to this heroic settlement, a place that will remain victorious no matter what happens to it tomorrow or the day after.

With dignity, the people of Dobrinja have demonstrated in an irrefutably concrete way why Sarajevo's future does not depend on begging for a pittance here and there, nor on appeals, complaints and grievances, or pointing a finger at the other side. Everything the future may bring is already within us, in today's relationships—in the strength to persevere, the will to survive, the capacity to share sorrows and moments of happiness. In the awareness that here no one lies to anyone, nor can there be coercion or deceit.

You can say what you want about the demagogy of old slogans like "equal stomachs," the "pernicious nature of theories of social justice," but in Dobrinja this "demagogy" and this "pernicious nature" have been vindicated, pulling people through their worst moments. For Dobrinja to have all it has today—despite the fact that its thoroughfares still run through cellars, bedrooms, garages, and rooftops, despite the fact that people are still buried there on the street and in backyards—their commanders had to eat the same tasteless rice in lukewarm water six months ago like everyone else. And they probably didn't have to. But if they hadn't, today the situation would be quite a bit different. Worse, of course. Like in many parts of what remains of Sarajevo. Particularly in the places that insisted on decorating heroes before the first shot was even fired. We know this story, the one about warriors whose greatness comes before the battle—we know it too well. Luckily, the average citizens of Dobrinja never recognized these "heroes," nor do they now. So there is hope.

NOT EVEN THE TREES
ARE SPARED

It has been an exceptionally calm day: only six dead and ten wounded. From the bullet-riddled window of my office, I watched some guys cut down one of the five big trees in front of our building. I remember when their foliage hid the view of the hills north of Sarajevo. For some reason, I believed those five giants might be spared, even though nothing and no one is spared here anymore. For days the noose has been tightening around them, and their departure will make us feel even lonelier in our ravaged building. Their end strikes me as tragic, almost more so than death by mortar shell, which, you'd say, takes a "real" life. Maybe that's because life has become so cheap in this unfortunate city, while trees can represent a little hope for us. It is hard to pin down, but they seemed to prove that things were still more or less normal, although I think you'd have a hard time trying to explain to anyone that people killing each other for no apparent reason is normal.

It hurts, too, that this giant tree wasn't cut down by people who are freezing, but by people who will sell it as firewood, at a premium, to those who *are* freezing.

But I suppose that's how things are now. The lie has

slithered in among us. Treason erodes us, speculation poisons us. The first snow reveals the tracks of these animals. There are profits to be made out of the suffering of others. What's worse, profit from misfortune is presented as a favor to the victim, to those defeated long ago.

There are people who are now beginning to deny their names and their origin. These poor bastards believe that this will save them. I never imagined there were so many Jews and Slovenians in this city; I only found out when their convoys began to leave Sarajevo. Many suddenly discovered that Jewish or Slovenian blood coursed strongly through their fathers' or grandfathers' veins, and more and more of them made this discovery as the departure date of the convoy drew closer. That's life. We don't have the energy left to indulge ourselves in malicious criticism of these conversions. And why should we? We'd be better off asking ourselves what we would do in their place.

What in fact would we do? Fortunately for me, most of the people around me have no doubts whatsoever. They are as determined to remain what and where they are as they have ever been. They all seem to share the same thought: one day this will be over, and there will be some mirrors left in town in which we will have to look at ourselves. And what shall we do then? Which bus would we depart on? With what collective passport, made out in whose name?

With tears in their eyes, such people give a frenetic standing ovation to our version of *Hair, Anno Domini 1992* at the Chamber Theatre. A moment of joy in the darkness— temporarily interrupted by the erratic generators running the stage lights—which gives rise to great hopes that moments like this will soon become more familiar.

Meanwhile, outside, our feet are cold, our hearts are cold. We get two hundred and thirty-three grams of bread per day, eight hundred grams of flour for twenty-five days, and also—to last us through the century—a package of feta cheese. The kerosene is running out; day by day our lamps get dimmer as they feebly resist the night into which the drunken *chetniks* want to plunge us, and the view from the little hills that once were parks grows more and more open.

The German mark has lost the battle against itself, or against potatoes and onions. Only incurable optimists still believe that they will be buried next to their families. And somewhere out there, far away, boxes are being taken out with colored balls and little lights as people sort out their Christmas decorations.

Here we sort out the memories of our lives, at least those of us who still have such memories. And we miss those giant trees, of which only stumps are left, cut as close to the ground as possible. The most efficient, though, are the people who have been enlarging our horizons. They know quite well the easiest ways to cut into the ground and seed it. No one needs to ask anymore just how deep a shell penetrates. Everything here has already reached a greater depth than one would have hoped. That's why, if nothing else, it is necessary to preserve your name and the name of your ancestors. Our children need at least that.

2 December 1992

CLOSE TO MADNESS

Okay, what's new this morning? No electricity, no water, no telephone. Last night? No sleep. Only this unseasonably blue sky and the cold, a cold growing steadily worse, from which there can be no excape. What isn't inescapable here? The worst of it, though, is that you can't even get away from yourself, from the blues that choke you from within, binding our thoughts and legs, our eyes. We no longer think about the war, the shells, the blood, the deaths, the way we thought about them at first. We've just become used to them as things that have always been with us, and which, simply, are part of our due.

Whether we admit it or not, more and more we've been thinking the same thought: can we get through this whole thing and stay sane? Who will make it, and who will go crazy? Until recently, half in jest but half seriously, we might have said, discreetly, that someone or other had "gone over the edge." You notice that someone has begun talking nonsense, that all he has on his mind is nonsense, and that he is getting ready to do something ridiculous. But today we don't talk about people like that anymore, and I know well why not. It is because we find ourselves, with increasing frequency, doing things that once would have astonished us or made us laugh. Which side of the thin line are we on? And how can we tell these days which side is better? What does it mean for us, here and now, to be on the right side of reason—when all sides are equally possible, even desirable?

Yesterday, while we had a little power, I watched the Novi Sad television newscast. What did I see? A creature wearing the Serb cap with its big shiny white eagles, and further adorned with a rifle, an ammunition belt, knives, and, inevitably, a beard. Impassively, this creature said that this is "a horribly and incredibly bloody and senseless war, a veritable genocide, incomprehensible to any normal person." Later, the *Srna* station in Pale broadcast a movie about Sarajevo in its heyday, underscored by a love song to the city and its beauties, which we—we who are here now—"have destroyed." Hard to decide which of these performances was the more nightmarish.

The day before yesterday, Nobel Laureate Elie Wiesel dropped in on us. He did the city in half an hour before going over to see Mladić at his crib in Lukavica, where he spent nine-tenths of his visit to Sarajevo. He reprimanded us gently for doing things "comparable to what they are doing over there." So really, where are the strands of sanity we are supposed to hold onto? Can anyone take it anymore?

Last summer, when the weather was fine, you could still find a secluded green spot and be alone, to gather your thoughts all by yourself. Today that is no longer possible.

We walk on top of one another in a single room, with some makeshift heater stoked up. We're breathing down each other's necks, listening to every incoherent utterance which we would never even think about noticing if things were just an iota more normal and we had someplace to go.

In just a few square meters, we've managed to accumulate a heap of varied neuroses, futile hopes, survival spasms. And that's how it is every day, with no hope of escape.

Nowhere to go except into the freezing cold or a hail of bullets. Who knows, perhaps the winter outside is the only place where reason has a chance to survive: white, cold, and infinitely silent. As long as a bullet doesn't come whistling along. But when you hear it whistling, that means it's already past. The one with your name on it you won't hear. Perhaps that is a blessing we have earned, who knows?

THE PRIZE AND THE PUNISHMENT

I hope I'll be forgiven, after all this time and all these Sarajevo war stories, if I'm professionally incorrect now, a bit pretentious, perhaps even lacking in political tact—but I'm going to tell you a little story about all of us who have been plunged into this madness, beginning with what at first might sound like a personal matter, though it really isn't particularly personal.

I got word from Paris that Reporters Without Borders had picked me as this year's laureate of their international prize, which, as they wrote, "is awarded to defenders of the dignity and liberty of the press" in times when professional journalists are under extremely heavy pressure from propaganda and politics. After they had told me the good news, they invited me to come to Paris the following Saturday to get the award at a big feast in honor of the recipients. They would take care of my ticket, and everything else. And that is just where this seemingly private episode of my war stories begins.

In spite of all kinds of unheard-of efforts by Reporters Without Borders, by friends known and unknown, by official and officious persons, ambassadors, ministers, councilors and journalists, I won't get to Paris on time; I might never get there.

Someone doesn't want to let me go. The good, but deceitful, side of the story will remain on paper with the kind invitation, and the truth about who we are, how they treat us, and what they do to us will stay put in its rightful place—in Camp Sarajevo, Prison Sarajevo, Sarajevo shame of the sated, pampered, and bloated, Sarajevo the sorrow from which we shall emerge one day, stronger, more dignified, and more honest than those who won't be able to look at themselves in the mirror after they see us.

To put it plainly, I can't leave Sarajevo at any price today, except through deceit, by bending my back right to the floor. Those who have something to tell this arrogant world are precisely those who can't leave: writers, journalists, intellectuals, actors. . . . They might be able to describe a reality in which we are not a band of savages who deserve nothing better than suffering, stench, and death, but that we are, or were until yesterday, people like you in the rest of Europe—though this may explain why Europe has been plagued by bombers and assassins. But their stories, which they would gladly tell to anyone, might upset a few people, maybe just a tiny bit—and now is never the time to get upset or have a bad conscience.

In the name of the "defense of the dignity and liberty of the press," as the Reporters Without Borders put it, this had to be written. As for the prize, what can I say? This is no time for prizes. One day, perhaps, it might serve some people, people outside of Sarajevo who have managed within themselves, for themselves, and facing themselves, to vanquish that monster of cultural degeneracy which allowed them to remain unmoved by the suffering of innocent and dignified people. That's why we won't leave. Our place is here, and their place is there. What would they do with our freedom? Maybe this had to be explained to them, once again.

NAMELESS HORROR

What wouldn't I give to know how all this will end! Do we still, after all that has happened, stand the slightest chance? Or is everything already lost? Is it futile to continue living in the hope that one day we will be vindicated, at the cost of our wounds? And will there be any more days, any more hope?

Today it is hard to fight back the tears, in these eyes that have almost run dry, after the news of what has happened to an eleven-year-old: Standing in a line for water in the vicinity of Pivara (a brewery in town), both his father and mother were killed by sniper fire. As I write, half the personnel of the hospital is engaged in the battle to save the life of his sister, a girl of seventeen.

After the shooting, this boy started to fetch and pour water over the bodies of his dead parents. He didn't want to stop even when his sister, seriously wounded, told him: "Stop, Berin, stop, they're dead."

What's with this water that we, curiously robotic and near exhaustion, have been carrying in buckets for months? And what kind of power have we been waiting for these forty days? What will we do with it, and it with us, if it comes back one day? Will it change anything for that woman who this morning slammed the door on a number of exhausted, thirsty people, as soon as the water supply was restored to her building?

Who will replant—and when—the thousands of trees we have lost? Who will ever be able to sit in the shade of the old oak tree in the park down the street, which for days has been attacked with hatchets and all kinds of knives, like the Lilliputians hacking away at Gulliver, to no avail?

I hear that Disney movies have been banned in Belgrade. I am convinced that what they need there is more Disney. They should be able to see Disney movies ten times a day. Then, perhaps, Berin's parents would still be alive.

Is it possible that things could change anymore? Isn't it too late for us, and for changes? It has become futile to speak, to write, to explain things to people who aren't here. I recently ran into an old friend who told me she has sworn never to speak of what has happened to us, if she survives, right up to the day she dies. Her father, who is over there, in the Far East, and whom she miraculously managed to telephone to wish a happy birthday, told her flatly: "How can you go on with these stories about snipers? No sniper on Mount Trebević could ever hit anything in the center of town. . . ."

That same day, a sniper killed a thirteen-year-old girl from a distance twice as long. But a father is a father. Just as our own eyes are our own eyes.

Today, in the rubble-strewn quarters of *Oslobodenje*, two spick-and-span officers of the British security forces came to see whether the container of gasoline we had managed to secure, with great effort, could be brought to fuel our generator. They found that it wouldn't be possible to have it carried here, conditions being too unsafe. "But we come here every day, in spite of the shooting. No one would ever think of saying it's impossible just because it's dangerous," we told the officers of the Kingdom's Armada. "But it's different for us," they said, and left. Right they were. So what does that make us? Second, third, fourth . . . ? Certainly not quite first-class. Nevertheless, we find it a bit hard to get used to that.

What will become of us? What dead bodies will we be rinsing with the fresh water that we have collected, drop by drop? And this is happening because we refuse to become cattle, a herd or mass of glands trained to function only *en masse*.

As a response to all this suffering, Afan Ramić has had an opening at an art gallery. His show is an attempt to escape from the fact that he buried his only son, and that the canvases he left at Grbavica have been burned. What more could they have taken from him? These days gallery openings aren't advertised, out of fear of the shooting idiots.

Nevertheless, everybody who was told was there, and for a moment it was the Sarajevo we used to know. There were Catholics and members of the Orthodox church, university professors and Communists, Muslims and soccer players, people of the moment, people of the past and the future, locksmiths and lathe turners, young girls and old duffers, officers and gentlemen, priests, some elegant dolls of "the other kind," parents and toddlers, café owners and painters, mathematicians and chauffeurs, musicians and drunks. All of them bringing their doubts, their worries, their sadness, but all joined together in one place, at Afan's new show: Sarajevans.

It felt good to be in the company of one's own, and it was reassuring, heartwarming. Because the trees keep growing without anybody's help, and the water around the city can't be stopped from flowing. The gathering proved to me that telephones aren't, after all, indispensable tools for those who can see clearly and who don't, to be honest, have a whole lot to say to one another. We know what is going on here.

Only, Berin will never again have a father or a mother. Let us pray for his sister, and never forget that prayer, and its origin. Its memory must be kept for our children, and their children. This is not a war. This is a horror that has no name. It is a black hole in the spectrum of all reasoned thought.

TO THE LAST BOSNIAN

After such incredible bloodshed, we have now reached the point we have been hearing about all year long—the realization of the Vance-Owen plan for Bosnia-Herzegovina, the plan that will divide this old Balkan country once and for all.

It is a plan that will allow the war to continue full blast, will encourage further destruction, and will sow the fear of crimes of every description.

In Bosnia, the Croats have now joined the Serb *chetniks* in adopting the same style of fascism as Milošević's men—one nation, one country, one leader. . . . A hysterical wave of chauvinism and Nazism is sweeping through Bosnia, sanctioned by the European countries whose inability to react has surpassed all limits, going even beyond shame.

A battle between good and evil has been joined here. Contrary to what the world's human, political, and military "Great Powerless Powers" have to say, what is at present happening in Bosnia has nothing to do with nationality or with religion, language, and heritage. Here the gates of hell have opened, and out of the darkness have emerged monsters—worse than monsters—capable of raping six-year-old girls, of burning people alive, of destroying age-old monuments.

But by destroying the mosques of Ferhadija and Ar-
naudija, they have not only destroyed a cultural heritage of
Islam: they have annihilated the soul of sacred places.

Those who are capable of such deeds are not welcome
here. You may remember a time half a century ago when
others like them arrived at midnight to round up and take
away millions of people who never returned. Those who
remained consoled themselves with the thought that it
could not happen to them, since they weren't Jews. The
next night they came again, looking for Communists, and
on the third night those who remained had nothing left to
console themselves with, because now it was their turn.

Here in Sarajevo, we have been deceived once again.
Promises of planes, food, and aid have been broken. Having lied to us, the criminals have continued to destroy Zepa,
Sarajevo, Mostar, Jablanica, and Goradze. As well as monuments, they have destroyed history, hope, and goodness. It
is their aim to destroy everything, down to the last Bosnian.
They will go on destroying until all that remains is evil,
hatred, nationalism, and fascism.

May God forgive them. We here, unimportant and
naive as we may be, will try to preserve in our souls at least
a trace of the sense of justice that we once had. We Sarajevans have been able to conquer hate. We pride ourselves
on being different in that respect.

15 June 1993

WORSE THAN A RESERVATION

Alija Izetbegović, the president of Bosnia-Herzegovina, a country recognized by the international community but now practically nonexistent, has recently rejected the idea of "protected zones" for Bosnian Muslims, saying that Bosnians are not Indians to be penned on reservations.

Technically speaking, Izetbegović is right. Charging over the hills, latter-day cowboys have chased these "Indians" off their lands. They have also burned down their homes, raped their women, and massacred their children. Now they will regroup and string barbed wire around a few isolated zones, herd the remaining Indians into these reservations, and be done with them once and for all.

In practical terms, however, Izetbegović is wrong when he compares Indian reservations to the protected zones proposed by a United Nations that no longer commands the respect of anyone. He is wrong, first of all, because the country occupied by the real-life cowboys, the United States, never belonged to just anybody, but historically always fell under the power of the strongest.

Since the days of the Far West, or so we have been told, many things have changed. That is why we, humble Europeans of Bosnia, ended up believing that now there *was* such a thing as the rule of law, that power was no longer solely a matter of brute force. This turns out not to be the case, and Izetbegović, as president of a nation, should have foreseen the present disastrous state of affairs.

Furthermore, the Indian reservations still exist today, and American Indians now have freedom of movement. This will not be the case for people in the protected zones. American Indians are, in fact, free to leave their reservations, to come and go—to the seaside, the mountains, the movies, or the supermarket. They are not forced to wait desperately for airplanes to bring them humanitarian aid, or for the opening of another corridor, as the Muslims would have to do.

Izetbegović's third mistake is that he does not consider how the Indians live on their American reservations. Had he bothered to take a closer look, he would have seen that they are free to work, to engage in business. But let us take a look at what constitutes, in effect, the first protected zone for Muslims, Srebrenica: thousands of people who have no idea what to do next packed into a small space, without work and without any foreseeable improvement in their deplorable condition. They stay home and stare at the walls—if they still have walls to stare at.

They are not given the chance to live lives of any dignity, or to work like everybody else; they are condemned to physical deterioration and a steady degradation. . . .

When Izetbegović spoke of Indian reservations, he must have thought he had found an appropriate analogue for the protected zones and other plans cooked up in the great American and European political kitchens. But he was wrong, and he insulted the cowboys of the Far West.

The protected zones are far worse than reservations. Having vanquished the Indians by force, the cowboys at least left them their liberty and human dignity. The international community has not deigned to grant these rights to Bosnians.

The Bosnians would surely forgive the world for a loss of territory, as the Indians have forgiven the cowboys. But the children of Bosnia will never be able to forgive the shame and degradation inflicted upon them. Europe will come to realize this, but, unfortunately, too late. It won't be "too late" for Bosnia, though, because Bosnia will no longer exist.

14 July 1993

GENTLEMEN AND COMRADES!

We Sarajevans are well aware that the world at large has grown tired of seeing images of horror on the television screen, images of a city dying of hunger and thirst, especially at this time of year when everybody is getting ready to go on vacation. Poor vacationers, they don't deserve to be subjected to scenes of such savagery.

Neither do we want these images to haunt your TV screens. To have all our misery and poverty captured by foreign television cameras only makes us feel worse. All we want, from the bottom of our hearts, is to be left alone. We don't want to be scrutinized by an indifferent world. This world has made us what we are today. It has destroyed us, but we won't allow it to steal our last shreds of dignity by filming us as if we were animals in a zoo.

So go on vacation, have a good time, all you big shots in New York and Geneva and Brussels and Strasbourg, and forget about the thousands of children now dying in Sarajevo.

Two days ago, the people of this city were reduced to drinking water from a river that serves as a sewer for the entire urban water system. By whatever means at their disposal, they then tried to boil this water, despite the extreme scarcity of firewood. The strongest and bravest

among us have started digging wells in our gardens, hoping
to find salvation underground, if nowhere else.

We have also been told that within a week, all incubators
for premature babies will be disconnected.

Today in Sarajevo one witnesses the depths of human
misery. . . . But there is an even worse human misery in
this world, that of the international community—for it is a
far greater misery for people to stand by and watch, in a
cold-blooded fashion, thousands of other people dying of
hunger and thirst.

In the name of what principles, what truth, what civilization do the mighty of this world allow this massacre to
continue? In the name of what policy and whose interests is
the suffering of some allowed to exceed the minimal standards of humanity that still exist in this world? What is now
happening in Sarajevo no longer has anything to do with
any policy or strategy, or with the French, the British, the
Russians, or the Americans.

It is quite simply the end of the world; and after this
terrible experience, everything will become possible again.

Water pumps and reservoirs situated less than five kilometers from the city could easily be protected by the Blue
Helmets. This would allow the inhabitants of Sarajevo to
survive with slightly greater dignity. But the Blue Helmets
are unwilling to do this. It is not their job.

Their job consists solely of passively observing the genocide, the persecution of thousands of children, and the
advance of the fascists on Sarajevo.

Messrs. Ghali, Clinton, Mitterrand, Yeltsin, Major, and
others: Know that it is you and you alone who are responsible for the deaths of thousands of children in Sarajevo.
First, because you have allowed aggressors to shoot them,

and second, because you have not given them the care and treatment they need. But the foundation you have built of lies and wrongdoing will not support you much longer.

The death of people from hunger and thirst in Europe at the end of the twentieth century is not the worst thing that can happen. Dying is only a passage to our final rest. You, on the other hand, will have to go on living with this crime on your conscience.

I would not like to trade places with you.

Gentlemen: Sarajevo is a good-sized city, and its weight will be a heavy burden on your conscience. I ask myself how you will explain to your own young children why you did nothing at a time when all that was asked of you was simple humanity.

The city dying of hunger and thirst, the city you could have saved without much effort, will speak for itself to your children.

THE CHILD HUNT

Here in Sarajevo we have witnessed incredible things in the course of this war, but the events of the past week have surpassed our worst nightmares. First of all, we were told to construct air-raid shelters because the bombardment, by the NATO air force, of Serb positions around Sarajevo was "imminent." Then, before more than a hundred journalists, an official UN spokesman calmly stated that Sarajevo was really not under siege, and that it was only the "warfare in central Bosnia" that created supply problems for our city. Later, the same sources informed us that the soldiers who had been besieging us for fifteen months had retreated from the surrounding hills, and still later, that the "humanitarian blockade of the city will be lifted." At the end of this same week, we saw and heard the most incredible thing of all: a veritable hunt for wounded children in Sarajevo hospitals. Without notice, without a chance to say goodbye to their parents, these children were whisked off to Britain and elsewhere in a spectacular action to evacuate them with military aircraft.

This provided the crowning touch to the nightmare. True, there may be a perfectly logical reason for each of these actions. The adversarial game between the Americans and the Europeans, in which it's our heads that are at stake, had reached impressive proportions. In their effort to prevent the air strikes favored by the Americans, the Europeans once again showed great ingenuity. In order to demonstrate that there was no reason for such an action, they came up with an argument that must strike every Sarajevan as the sheerest fantasy: no need to panic, Sarajevo really isn't under siege.

However, in this suddenly "liberated" city, there now were over one hundred and sixty foreign journalists who suddenly found themselves deprived of their anticipated show. The French and English Blue Helmets declared that since Sarajevo was not under siege, the air strikes would not take place after all, so the journalists, who had come here to cover the action, looked around for something else to report. Word of a seriously wounded young girl sent dozens of them on a chase for "their child," turning her evacuation from Sarajevo into a circus.

The medical community of Sarajevo watched this chase, initiated by powerful television networks and newspapers, in astonishment. How was it possible to accomplish in a single day what had been unimaginable for so long? Where did all this money come from, this willingness to launch an operation a thousand times more expensive than the fuel the hospitals had been lacking for months? Owing to that lack of fuel, the most complicated surgical operations had been performed by candlelight. . . . Why was it necessary to use military planes to transport these children, if Sarajevo no longer was under siege? And had it not been proclaimed that the wounded should be treated here, and not evacuated? True, in order to treat them here it would be necessary to improve conditions in Sarajevo, and the powers that be had not been helpful in that respect.

Once again, these events have shown us only what we already knew. The politics of the great powers and the politics of foreign television networks and newspapers allow them to do what they will with poor Sarajevo. Our city has been reduced to the status of a zoo. Personally, I am delighted to hear the news that Sarajevo isn't under siege. That means I can go wherever I want whenever I want; that I'm carrying fifty liters of water every day just to entertain myself; and that if I manage to have a meal only every other day, this is not because there is not food but because I don't want to eat any more than that. Furthermore, it reassures me to know that all the people killed in the last few days were not killed by shells fired from the hills; they simply committed suicide for their own pleasure.

At first we thought that no one understood Sarajevo at all. Then we believed that it was all a matter of great-power politics, and that we simply did not fit into that scheme. Today we know that the world is perverse, that it relishes our plight with a degree of sadism. The training of the circus animals has reached new heights. I only hope that the trainers don't lose control, and that the situation doesn't become too dangerous for the audience to watch.

WE'LL DIE TOGETHER
AND IN LOVE

Those of us who live in Sarajevo have seen nothing more absurd during the course of this disgusting war than the incessant flights of NATO's awesome warplanes as they cruise over our city. We've watched them now for months, and our feelings have turned from curiosity and hope—when we first heard their thundering voices over Bosnia—to cynicism.

A couple of days ago, I watched an old woman drag a branch she'd managed to chop from one of our few remaining trees. After the deafening roar of the Phantoms had passed, she waved scornfully toward the sky and shouted, "Go back home, you cowards, and bother your own mothers! Shake your own mothers' windows!"

There is no reason to believe that these flights evoke anything other than smiles from the snipers in the hills. Who could be frightened by the empty threats made in Brussels?

But in Sarajevo, we are spending our last reserves of hope in an effort to survive until the final act draws to a close. Even those who had been considered brave and optimistic, who refused to scurry in fear across the street but continued to stride nonchalantly, are now hanging on by a thread. Fear has entered every pore. We can no longer sleep. There is nowhere left to hide from the shells that have systematically narrowed the circle around every one of us.

The futile precautions we all go through—calculating where the next shell will fall, listening carefully for the whistling of passing shells—have brought even yesterday's heroes to ruins. In just the last few weeks, shrapnel has found its way to a child asleep in bed, a young woman setting the table for her first wedding anniversary, an old man alone in his kitchen drinking tea, an entire family of six.

At dusk, on what had been a beautiful day, I saw a car heading toward the hospital; hanging out the back door were the legs of a man who had been hit by a sniper bullet. The car passed a little girl tossing a stick for her dog. A few minutes later, only 300 meters away, a shell took a whole floor off a gorgeous, old house. The girl and the dog continued playing as if nothing had happened.

And so it continues, word by word, story by story, death by death. Near the grave of my father, whom I buried on the tenth of January, fifty-six new graves appeared within three days.

My father and I were together the day before he died, and, as if he sensed he was about to depart, he told me of his three unfulfillable wishes: that he would see his grandchildren again; that he would see his birthplace, Mostar, again; and that he would play his violin again. The violin had been demolished a few days earlier when a shell exploded nearby. But at least I know where his grave is, and with my friends I was able to bury him. Not everyone is so lucky.

My father was lucky enough to die of "natural causes." Of course, the fifty-six new graves all belong to people who died of "natural causes": from sickness or shelling, from a sniper's bullet or a hand grenade. If these deaths had not been of natural causes, it would have been possible to stop them. But those who want to stop the dying can't; and those who can don't want to—for reasons known only to themselves.

Since the war began, Sarajevo's Jews have steadily been leaving the city. There have been Jews here for 500 years. This has been their home, and they have had as much right to it as anyone. They are being driven from Sarajevo not only by the evil committed against us all but also by the world's indifference.

The Jews are being forced to abandon the city by officials in Belgrade and Zagreb. These men are well aware that if all the Jews depart, it would signal the destruction of one of the four pillars on which Sarajevo has stood, one of the communities, along with those of the Muslims, Serbs, and Croats, that has given the city its flavor. Then it would be easier to destroy one of the three that remain. And then one of the two. And finally, the last pillar propping up civil humanity, tolerance, and cosmopolitan life will fall.

In the end, all that remains will be a vast, aching hole whose bottom will be found in the souls of those who could have acted to prevent this from happening but chose not to.

Still, until that moment, Sarajevo will do its best to continue as it always has. Last month we celebrated the Serbian Orthodox Christmas holiday, and it went very well. For whom? For all the Sarajevans who celebrated it. And many did.

A group of our soccer players had a parting match with some United Nations troops who are being sent back home. They have been here too long and have begun to understand all too well what is going on in our city, so replacements are being shipped in. Whoever begins to comprehend what is happening in Sarajevo had better be flown home immediately. Then a flood of fresh faces arrives, new recruits who are completely confused by our situation and who think that "all three sides" are equally to blame for this madness—and who think that this is a civil war rather than genocide.

The Sarajevan players felt lousy about the likelihood of trouncing the UN soccer team in their last match together—even though they had always won the lopsided games before—so the game ended in a tie. The troops have had enough troubles to deal with: they've seen too much, they're haunted by enough nightmares. At least they should travel in peace. At the end of the game, one woman asked whether she should prepare sandwiches for their trip. It would be sinful to let them leave on an empty stomach.

Besides, all of us Sarajevans are fully sated with things as they are. Our lives, humanitarian aid, planes booming overhead. It's all fine by us. It's the world out there, beyond our walls, that is less than inspiring.

That's why we're satisfied to remain in Sarajevo, our city that we refuse to abandon. We don't hate you, those of you outside Sarajevo. We just take pity on those of you who have accepted this latest form of totalitarianism that lays a civilization to waste. Most likely, in Sarajevo we'll die together and in love. The fascists will die alone and in hatred. This is no small difference.

PLAYING HOST TO SOME DUBIOUS GUESTS

Last Monday morning, when the promised NATO air strikes against Serbian guns turned into a big nothing—just as we figured—a white armored personnel carrier with UN markings came through the center of town. It went down Marshal Tito Street, turning toward the presidency building before coming to a stop. Then the back doors opened and from the black innards, potatoes began falling out on the sidewalk, at the feet of astonished pedestrians. As the carrier turned on its way, more and more potatoes came tumbling down, rolling every which way. At first the pedestrians turned cautiously, looking this way and that to see whether anyone was watching. Then, almost in a panic, people began running and bending, grabbing at potatoes in the snow. A cyclist fell off his bike as he tried to stop abruptly at the spot where the most potatoes were. A woman began stuffing potatoes in her bosom; a couple of guys grabbed at a torn nylon sack that had drifted in with the wind; a ten-year-old kid took off his jacket to make a bag that he kept filling and filling.

About ten people stood around mutely staring at this spectacle. Only one very distinguished-looking woman, her white, wrinkled face emanating its own brand of aristocracy, quietly uttered, "There, freedom has come." A tear rolled down her cheek. Meanwhile, the local TV station replayed the reports that had been broadcast over "Serbian" television the night before; showing that Pale, where the bloody siege of Sarajevo has been engineered for nearly seven hundred days, seems an outburst of joy and happiness: "The Russians have come!" It was hard to tell who did more kissing, whose hands were stiffer from repeatedly raising three fingers in the sign of victory and greeting: the crazed Serb hosts whose "historical Orthodox allies" had finally come to their aid or the exalted Russians who did nothing to hide their sense of triumph.

It was also just around then that we found out about the announcement made by Manfred Wörner, the general-secretary of NATO: "The victors here, above all, are the citizens of Sarajevo." I ran into Afan Ramić, the artist, on the street that morning, and he said, looking at me quite seriously after seeing Wörner's statement in *Oslobodenje,* "If it doesn't beat all hell, they always hide things from me whenever I come out the winner." The Indi Cafe, better known as Asha's Place, was closed, but a sign was still on the door: WE WILL BE HOLDING A CELEBRATION TO FOLLOW THE NATO ATTACK ON MONDAY. That afternoon there was no celebration, the sign disappeared and the cafe didn't open again until the following day. Nearby at Bisera's bar, things looked like a get-together after a funeral. "My God, how we've been humiliated by the Russians. What a disgrace," Bisera mused, almost as if she were saying it to herself.

"Liberated Sarajevo" seemed almost as if it didn't want to admit to itself that its ears were perked for those planes of Monday, planes whose one and only mission—at least as far as we were concerned—was to show those holding us hostage from the hills that someone stronger existed. To show them for just an instant that force can counteract force, that there is no heroism in killing women and children, that there is no heroism in depriving the hungry and thirsty, the freezing and the sick, of electricity and water.

Many who listened for sounds in the sky that morning when the potatoes went rolling along Marshal Tito Street simply declared that "NATO is afraid of Russia." Those inclined to mix in politics went a step further: it wasn't NATO getting scared but the West wishing to save Boris Yeltsin, for the umpteenth time. This time Yeltsin was being saved from Vladimir Zhirinovsky, the KGB, and some shadowy Russian generals who don't exactly have a subtle grasp of all "the new historical realities." But most people no longer felt the need to analyze the motives of their supposed saviors, and they simply sneered as they went by the regiments of foreign journalists assaulting pedestrians as they shoved microphones in their noses and cameras in their faces, asking them astonishing questions: "What do you think now? What are your hopes? Are you happy? Who is the winner here?" One Sarajevan answered sharply and laconically, "The Russians won."

And they did. Under the wings of the doctrines expounded by Slobodon Milošević and Radovan Karadžić about the need "to defend the Western borders of Orthodox Christianity" right here, in Bosnia, the Russians managed to assume a position they had only dreamed about for a long time. And what's more, they have finally gained access to the "warm sea," the Adriatic. Most ironic, they gained the moral upper hand, to the detriment of NATO, which forfeited any of the moral stature it might have once held.

At Asha's Place, a guy just started in pointlessly over his beer: "And what would you think if instead of the Russians, the Turks had come in to take over the Serb positions around Sarajevo? They're part of NATO, too."

"What the hell are you asking *us* for? Go ask Manfred Wörner, or Yeltsin. They're the bigwigs," snapped Asha, cleaning his pipe. "As far as we're concerned, from now on the only person worth turning to is Yeltsin. Maybe later on it'll be Zhirinovsky," concluded Asha, frantically trying to light his pipe with a lighter that had the UN insignia on it. No go. I guess there wasn't any flint left.

BACK ON TRACK

Sometime last summer, when we used to try to imagine the day when everything would finally stop and we could head south, toward the sea, one of my friends said: "As far as I'm concerned, I'll know the war is over when the trolleys start running again and, like in the old days, I can get on the Number Two and take it to the end of the line, right to Villa Čengić. And we can pass all the way across 'Sniper's Avenue,' but no one will be shooting at us."

We laughed then, looking over the twisted tracks, the fallen power lines, the wrecked and burned-out trolleys. The trolleys remained exactly where grenade and mortar shells had stopped them dead in their tracks in May of 1992. It seemed like everything else—the end of the war, a return to normal life—would come before the trolleys started running again. We figured that we'd get to the sea by car, or maybe even somewhere farther by plane, before we'd be able to make it to Villa Čengić on the Number 2 red line.

Things turned out differently. The conflict made fools of us again. When it comes to forecasting war and peace, politics and life, we have to admit, once more, that we're complete amateurs. The trolley is running. The tracks have been straightened out. The power lines have been put up and a few red cars, in mint condition, have been hauled out from God knows where. But none of this has anything to do with the end of the war we had imagined. And it has nothing to do with what our trip on the Number 2 would have meant. There is still no peace waiting for us at Villa Čengić.

What stands out most about the Number 2, as it makes its way through dead neighborhoods, is the route's senselessness. The trip is nothing more than movement from one place to another within the same concentration camp, the same prison. Once upon a time we used to sit in the Number 2 and head down to Baščaršigja, the heart of the Old Town of Sarajevo. Today the area is just a gaping hole, empty and calm. We used to get on the Number 1 and head for the railroad station and then go on from there, by train, to other places. Like normal people. Now there are no trains; there isn't even a railroad station. If they start the Number 1 again, what good will it be if it only serves the same bogus purpose as the Number 2? There were times when we used to pile into the Number 3 and somehow make it to Ilidža. And from there we could go wherever our hearts desired: down the old tree-lined avenue to the source of the Bosnia River, up to Mt. Igman or even to nowhere in particular. Thanks to the world's kindness and affection, Ilidža now belongs to "Them"; it is at the other end of the world, somewhere on another planet. You can't get there, as everyone well knows, by trolley. A revived Number 3 won't do us much good either.

The Number 2 is off and running, and everything else stays still, with very little hope for change. What a blunder it was to think that, one day, a trolley would take us to freedom. For the rest of the world—especially for the politicians and diplomats who try to get us to accept their lies, who try to get us to tell the world how happy we are—the resurrected trolley is a triumph. But what is it to us? How can we even begin to explain that we've always liked going to Ilidža, the railroad station, Mostar, the sea? And that we'd much rather go to these places on foot than have the ability to "freely" roll to nowhere on a trolley. As the Number 2 stops at every station on its aborted route across nothing, it creates an illusion that is equally senseless, revolting, and desperate.

Of course, it isn't easy trying to explain this to people who think that the only aim in life is to fill your stomach and your pockets, and that you can be as happy as a cow in five square meters of living space as long as you have your mercy provisions—the gift of a "landlord" or humanitarian organization. It's also tough to put a damper on the warm feelings of all those who helped get "Operation Trolley" underway by sending money, technicians, and even cameramen, just to make sure it was recorded for posterity. The "international community" also kept its honor intact and showed its strength, so its leaders would have good reason for a victorious toast over a glass of whiskey: A great nightmare no longer bears down on them in quite the same way or in quite the same place. That nightmare hopped onto the red line, Sarajevo's Number 2, and is making the rounds now.

But it's slightly more difficult to sell this story to those in Sarajevo who are still using their own heads to think with, something that may constitute this disobedient city's gravest sin. A few days ago Afan Ramić was talking with some people from Japan who had come to visit his studio, which is in an abandoned building that used to be a printing plant. They were a fine bunch, very serious, dignified, and sincere. They listened carefully, spoke carefully, and made offers even more carefully. For hours they studied the canvases, took pictures of the works. Then, with great tact and meticulously chosen words, they conveyed a message to the painter: the TV station, as well as their government, would be honored if he, the Sarajevan artist Afan Ramić, would come to Japan with his paintings. There would be exhibitions and all expenses would be paid. In short, they saw no problems except, of course, whether this "extremely interesting" painter would be willing to accept their invitation. Would this trip upset any other plans he might have made? Did he find the concept to his liking? Were there any special conditions that needed to be met?

"I looked at them for a while without really knowing what to say. I wasn't really sure, to tell you the truth, whether they were pulling my leg or whether they were serious," Afan said later. "I always admired the Japanese for their seriousness. Could it be that after seven hundred days of imprisonment, hunger, personal tragedy, and every other kind of misery imaginable, they were really asking me whether or not I wanted to go to Japan and have a show? And what's more, did they have any idea what they were saying when they claimed that everything would be OK as far as traveling was concerned? Then I decided to ask them what, around here, always ends up being the most important question: 'That's all well and good as far as Tokyo and Osaka go; I have no doubt that it's also nice in Nagoya and Yokohama, but how am I going to get past the Serb barricades on Ilidža?' I got the feeling that they felt confused and didn't quite grasp what

I was asking them. I actually began to feel sorry for them. Then I said, more to myself, 'Forget about it, don't worry, I'll get to Ilidža by trolley.'"

The Japanese went off happy that they had gotten Afan to come to their country. The painter was left to wait for the trolley to Ilidža, or some other mode of transportation the international community could arrange. After all, when you get past Ilidža and that last barricade, everything else is a lot easier. From there to Japan isn't far at all.

PLUNDERING HISTORY

I'll never forget that remarkable phrase uttered over the phone to Radovan Karadžić, the self-proclaimed leader of "all the Serbs of Bosnia-Herzegovina." The message was delivered, right at the very beginning of this horror, by Dobrica Ćosić, the then-president of the yet-to-be-recognized "Yugoslavia." "We have to do everything we can," he said, "in order to make possible what seemed impossible yesterday." That sentence alone has become the key foundation upon which the war in our country—if one can even refer to it as a war—continues to be waged.

Everything in the former Yugoslavia, as well as in Bosnia, has been made possible. Whatever anyone has a mind to do, regardless of how unlikely or insane it might seem, is possible. That is, insofar as those worldy politicians out there who cut the deck over life and death, reason and madness, good and evil, see fit. Nothing is sacred. No world order or "logical" sequence of events is even conceivable. We are confronted by an abyss which pulls in everything that had, at least until now, been considered of some worth: reason, logic, and truth, for instance.

Although Sarajevans no longer believe in anything or anyone, they continue to lunge for the few thousand copies of *Oslobodenje* that, despite everything, we still manage to get out on the streets every day. Consider, then, the sentiments induced by an item that came into the "offices" of *Oslobodenje*, stating that Radovan Karadžić and his team of propaganda experts had started a daily newspaper in Pale, the very place from which the siege of Bosnia is being orchestrated. The paper is called *Oslobodenje*, just like ours: a paper in which we've put whatever was left of our lives, whatever we still believe in, whatever keeps us going.

At first, we figured that those "up there" in the hills only wanted to mix people up, to make things a little tougher for us to swallow and to throw yet another monkey wrench into our already hopeless conditions for survival. But we soon realized that we weren't fully prepared for a scam of this scale. The lunacy cooked up by them was greater than anything we could have even imagined. In their introductory "statement of purpose," they wrote that this was not at all "another newspaper" and that "no other *Oslobodenje* exists." This, as they put it, "is the one and only *Oslobodenje*" and "it rightfully belongs to us, in Pale." According to them, we down here in Sarajevo, we're the ones who've stolen *Oslobodenje* from its rightful owners and occupied it since the beginning of the war; they are simply bringing it back to where it belongs. When asked about *Oslobodenje*'s crucial role as a voice against fascism for the past fifty years, their answer was in keeping with the cynicism and hypocrisy that has surrounded us for over two years now. "Naturally," they answered, "*Oslobodenje* remains anti-fascist, just as it has always been. Even now we're fighting against the fascists in Sarajevo, we're fighting for the freedom and democracy of the city. That's why we've got to use missiles against them. In the war against fascism, you've got to use everything at your disposal."

That, believe it or not, is it. They want to steal our newspaper and, failing that, they at least want to declare us the fascists. Everything that had truly been impossible until yesterday has now, as you can see, become possible. Karadžić listened to Ćosić, and the world listened to both of them. The only thing left for us now is to wait for that moment when someone in this sad world of ours will declare the murdered children of Sarajevo, Goradze, or Foča to be war criminals; when arrest warrants are issued for the former inmates of concentration camps; and, finally, when the coveted decision regarding massive airstrikes by NATO will be carried out—on the citizens of Sarajevo.

There's nothing further to report. Everything seems quite pointless. It's kind of tragic being an inhabitant of this planet, at the end of the Twentieth Century.

CHRONOLOGY OF EVENTS

1987 Rise of Slobodon Milošević.

1989 **February–March:** Serbian police force invades Kosovo; shortly thereafter federal army units are sent in. The Serbian constitution is changed, removing the autonomous status of Kosovo and making it part of Serbia.

November: The Berlin Wall comes down.

1990 **January:** Slovenian communists walk out of the last congress of the League of Communists of Yugoslavia.

March–April: Multi-party elections in Croatia and Slovenia.

August–October: Revolt of Krajina Serbs.

September: Referendum on autonomy of Serbs in Croatia.

1991 **March:** First demonstration staged by the Serb opposition put down by force in Belgrade.

June: Slovenia and Croatia declare their independence. The Yugoslav Federal army intervenes in Slovenia.

July: European mediation in the conflict begins; a three-month moratorium on Slovenian and Croat independence; retreat of the federal army from Slovenia.

August: Massive attacks by the federal army and Serb paramilitary forces on Croatia.

September: Opening of the Peace Conference in The Hague. Referendum on Macedonian independence. Proclamation of autonomous Serb regions in Bosnia-Herzegovina. Resolution Number 713 of the United Nations Security Council imposing an arms embargo on Yugoslavia.

October: Destruction of Ravno in Herzegovina by the federal army; Siege of Dubrovnik, Croatia.

November: Fall of Vukovar, Croatia.

December: Bosnian Parliament discusses independence declaration.

1992 **January:** Report of European Commission's Arbitration Commission. Recognition of Slovenia and Croatia by the European Community.

February: Referendum on the independence of Bosnia-Herzegovina.

March: Brussels Conference on the future of Bosnia-Herzegovina. Recognition of Bosnia-Herzegovina by the European Community. The inhabitants of Sarajevo demonstrate against the war. First attacks by the federal army and Serbian nationalist forces on Bosnian villages. Bombardment of Sarajevo begins.

May: The government of Bosnia-Herzegovina appeals for foreign military intervention. Slovenia, Croatia, and Bosnia-Herzegovina are admitted to the United Nations. The UN Security Council imposes an embargo on trade, oil, and air traffic on Serbia and Montenegro. Ethnic cleansing by Serbs made public by Haris Silajdžić. Kosovo votes to secede from Serbia.

June: One thousand Blue Helmets take up positions at Butmir airport in Sarajevo to protect the airlift. The presidency of Bosnia-Herzegovina declares a state of war and general mobilization. Dobrica Ćosić becomes president of former Yugoslavia.

July: Serbs cut through strategic corridor to Krajina.

August: The world learns of the existence of concentration camps in Bosnia-Herzegovina (the detainees are mostly Muslims and Croats). Security council resolutions 770 and 771 authorize the use of force to protect convoys carrying humanitarian aid to Bosnia-Herzegovina. London Conference opens.

September: Massive displacement of Muslims in the name of "ethnic cleansing" continues.

October: Security Council resolution 781 forbids any invasion of Bosnian air space by planes of any air force other than those employed by the UN and countries participating in the airlift.

December: Médicins Sans Frontières denounces the creation of new detention camps by the Serbs in Bosnia and demands an inquiry by the UN and the International Red Cross. Slobodon Milošević wins the presidential election in Serbia. Vance-Owen plan to divide Bosnia-Herzegovina into ten autonomous provinces is prepared.

1993 **January:** Vance-Owen plan presented. Fighting continues in Bosnia-Herzegovina. Hakija Turaijlić, Deputy Prime Minister of Bosnia, is assassinated by Serb forces while in a vehicle belonging to the Blue Helmets.

February: The Geneva talks resume; the US adopts the Vance-Owen plan. The UN Security Council unanimously adopts Resolution 808, which calls for the establishment of an international tribunal to put war criminals from the former Yugoslavia on trial. New federal army units enter Bosnia-Herzegovina.

March: The US airdrops packages of food and medical supplies in eastern Bosnia. Bosnian President Izetbegović signs the Vance-Owen peace plan, which is accepted by the Bosnian Croats but later rejected by the Bosnian Serb parliament. The Security Council adopts Resolution 816 authorizing the use of force to enforce the no-fly zone over Bosnia-Herzegovina.

April: Croatian nationalists attack the Muslim town of Jablanica, while on the same day Srebenica, which was taken by Serbian nationalists, is declared a "safe haven" by the UN. The UN Security Council tightens economic sanctions against Serbia while fighting intensifies between Bosnian Serbs and Croats.

May: The UN Security Council agrees on a "joint action program" that rules out intervention in Serbian controlled territory and proposes creating "safe havens" for the 1,200,000 Bosnian Muslims.

June: Lord Owen declares the Vance-Owen Plan dead. The Serbian nationalists launch a heavy offensive against Gorazde, one of the UN-declared "safe havens."

July: Serbian nationalist forces tighten their grip on Sarajevo and launch offensives against two strategic mountains outside the city. A tripartite division of Bosnia-Herzegovina is promoted in a new round of Geneva talks.

August: Mount Igman falls to Serbian nationalists. Threatened by the possibility of air strikes, the Serbian forces withdraw from Igman and Bjelasnica in the weeks that follow. Izetbegović agrees to consider the Owen-Stoltenberg proposal for the division of Bosnia.

September: Fikret Abdić, a member of the Bosnian presidency (soon expelled), declares the region of West Bosnia autonomous. Bosnian parliament rejects the Owen-Stoltenberg plan.

October: Fikret Abdić signs a pact with Bosnian Croats and then with Bosnian Serbs.

1994 February: New massacre at Sarajevo marketplace. NATO threatens air strikes. Russia announces deployment of peace-keeping forces in Bosnia. Serbian forces withdraw from perimeter of Sarajevo. Bosnian Government and Croatian Defense Council Com-

manders agree on cease-fire accord. Four Bosnian
Serb aircraft violate the UN ban on military aircraft
over Bosnia and are downed by NATO fighters.

March: Serbs continue bombardment of Maglaj in
northern Bosnia. Bosnian Serb and Bosnian government military leaders sign a UN-sponsored agreement on limited civilian movement in the Sarajevo
area. Bosnian Croatian Representative Krešimir
Zubac and Bosnian Premier Haris Silajdžić sign an
agreement to link areas of Bosnia-Herzegovina with
Bosnian Muslim and Bosnian Croatian majorities in a
federation. Simultaneously, President Alija Izetbegović of Bosnia-Herzegovina and President Franjo
Tudman of Croatia sign an agreement to link Bosnia-
Herzegovina and Croatia in a confederation. Bosnian Serb forces begin concentrated bombardment
of Gorazde.

April: Bosnian Serb forces break through Bosnian
government lines at Gorazde. US Secretary of State
Warren Christopher calls for deployment of 1,000
Ukrainian peacekeepers to the town; NATO planes
bomb Bosnian Serb positions. Western news agencies
report Serbian shelling of Sarajevo in violation of
UN-sponsored agreements. Bosnian Serb forces
begin to pull back after the UN Security Council
issues an ultimatum, but reportedly maintain troops
in southern Gorazde.

May: UN observers arrive near Brcko to head off a
battle for the strategic corridor connecting Serbian
occupied lands in northwestern Bosnia and the Croatian Krajina with Serbia proper. Bosnian Prime Minister Haris Silajdžić demands the removal of UN
envoy Yasushi Akashi after Akashi allows Serbian
tanks to pass through the Sarajevo exclusion zone
toward Herzegovina. The United States Senate

passes the Dole-Lieberman amendment to unilaterally lift the United Nations Arms Embargo. President Alija Izetbegović announces that Bosnia may not participate in scheduled peace negotiations unless Serbian forces withdraw completely from Gorazde. Bosnian parliament officially elects the Bosnian Croat Kresimir Zubac as president of the Bosnian Muslim-Croat federation and Bosnian Muslim Ejup Ganic as vice president. New fighting breaks out between Bosnian government and Serb forces throughout northern and western Bosnia.

June: Though scheduled Bosnian peace talks are suspended because of Serbian failure to withdraw from Gorazde, cease-fire talks soon begin at Geneva. Bosnian Muslim, Croat, and Serb representatives reach an agreement on a month-long cease-fire beginning June 10th. The United States House of Representatives passes the MacCloskey amendment calling on the United States government to unilaterally lift the United Nations arms embargo against Bosnia. UN officials report continued "ethnic cleansing" of non-Serbs in the Bosnian Serb controlled area of Banja Luka. Armed conflict in Bosnia is reported to be more intense than before the cease-fire agreement. The United States, its European allies, and Russia agree on a map for a peace settlement in Bosnia. Diplomats fear that a new Bosnian and Croatian military alliance will try to close the Serbian corridor across northern Bosnia. Europeans and Russians threaten the Bosnian and Croatian side with a lifting of economic sanctions on Serbia and the Serbian side with a lifting of the arms embargo on the Bosnian Muslim-Croatian federation.

GLOSSARY OF
KEY PERSONS, PLACES,
AND ORGANIZATIONS

Banja Luka: A city in northwest Bosnia under occupation by Serbian nationalist forces.

Boras, Franjo: Croatian member of the Bosnian Presidency.

Bosanski Brod: A city on the Sara River north of Sarajevo destroyed early in the war.

Bulatović, Momir: President of Montenegro.

Butmir: Site of the airport in the suburbs outside Sarajevo.

Carrington, Lord Peter: Chairman of the International Conference on the former Yugoslavia.

Ćosić, Dobrica: President of the former Yugoslavia through June 1993.

Croatian Defense Council (HVO): A Croatian nationalist militia.

Croatian Defense Forces (HOS): A Croatian nationalist militia.

Dobrinja: A suburb of Sarajevo isolated through much of 1992 by Serbian nationalist forces.

Elektroprivreda: Electricity Company of Bosnia.

Grbavica: A district of Sarajevo under Serbian nationalist control.

Grebo, Zdravko: Professor at the Law School of Sarajevo.

Green Berets: A militia which was formed at the beginning of the war to defend Bosnia.

High Commission for Refugees (UNHCR): A United Nations organization based in Geneva.

Higijenski Zavod: The Department of Health in Sarajevo.

Hrasno: A district in Sarajevo.

Ibrisimovic, Nedzad: a young Bosnian writer of fiction.

Ilidža: A district in Sarajevo

Izetbegović, Alija: President of the Presidency of Bosnia-Herzegovina.

Jahorina: A mountain east of Sarajevo, a site of ski events in the 1984 Olympics.

Karadžić, Radovan: President of the Bosnian Serb Parliament.

Kljujic, Stjepan: Leader of the Croatian members of the Bosnian parliament at the beginning of the war.

Koševo: A district in Sarajevo.

MacKenzie, General Louis: Canadian commander of the UNPROFOR forces.

Miljacka: a river that flows through the center of Sarajevo.

Milošević, Slobodan: President of Serbia.

Mladić, Ratko: The commander of the Bosnian Serb armed forces.

Mojmilo: The hill between the suburb of Dobrinja and the airport outside Sarajevo.

Mostar: a city in Herzegovina, once popular among tourists.

Nedžarići: A district in Sarajevo.

Novi Sad: A city in Vojvodina.

Pale: A village east of Sarajevo, the site of the Bosnian Serb Parliament.

Panić, General Zivota: Chief of staff of the army of the former Yugoslavia.

Plavsić, Biljana: A top aide to Karadžić and a member of the Bosnian Serb Parliament.

Romanija: A mountain northeast of Sarajevo.

Serb Democrat Party (SDS): Official party of the Bosnian Serb nationalists.

Šešelj, Vojislav: Leader of the ultra-nationalist Serbian Radical Party.

Sidran, Avdo: Poet and author of the screenplay for *When Father Was Away on Business*.

Stup: A district in Sarajevo.

Trebević: A hill outside of Sarajevo.

Unioninvest: A Sarajevan air-conditioning firm.

UNPROFOR: The United Nations peace-keeping forces.

Valter Perić: The Electricity Company of Sarajevo.

Vlašić: A mountain in the region outside of Sarajevo.